PERSONAL MEMOIRS

BOBBI SMITH

WestBow Press books may be ordered through booksellers or by contacting:

WestBow Press
A Division of Thomas Nelson & Zondervan
1663 Liberty Drive
Bloomington, IN 47403
www.westbowpress.com
844-714-3454

ISBN: 978-1-6642-1049-3 (sc)
ISBN: 978-1-6642-1048-6 (e)

Print information available on the last page.

WestBow Press rev. date: 11/03/2020

ACKNOWLEDGEMENT

I want to first, express gratitude to my parents for teaching me to recognize the value of an individual, regardless of their material wealth. I want to thank each of my siblings for remaining close to me, taking part in my childhood and imparting Christian ethics into my young life. Thank you for participating in, and helping to develop my strengths, and to also teach me to recognize my weaknesses and ask for help.

Thanks to my siblings for reinforcing some of my memories, especially to my brother Mick, for assisting me with the timeline and the names of past family and friends.

Thanks to my friend, Connie Edwards for editing my manuscript, so that I may share my story with others.

I give thanks to God for those who directed me as a young girl, encouraged and nurtured me during the years when I needed their guidance. I thank those "blue haired" ladies at church for drawing me close and instructing me in His Word.

Most of all, I give praise to God, who guided me with His gentle hand, and at the age of fourteen, gave me the free gift of Salvation through the shed blood of His Son. He gave me a purpose and I shall declare His love through the Good News for the rest of my life. I hope that the readers might see the ways in which His hand has been upon me throughout my journey.

INTRODUCTION

The young girl sat down on the steps of the back porch as she wrapped her arm around the family dog. She listened closely for the whistle sounding exactly at noon from the Wabash Railroad Round-House. The train was right on time as it entered the small railroad town, moving along the tracks through her neighborhood, and on past her house. Her dad joked that the conductors always called him to synchronize their clocks with his Elgin railroad watch.

She was fascinated by an occasional hand-car, which was a simple track vehicle used for maintaining the proper condition of the rails within a few mile section of the tracks. It consisted of a platform built on four flat rimmed wheels which was propelled by hand power. This small railed vehicle was driven by two men seated opposite one another, one in the front and one in the back, taking turns pumping up and down, one after the other. Their pumping action drove the movement of the vehicle. Rods, gears, and cranks enabled the single car to move smoothly. She watched closely, as the operators of the vehicle would often wave to her.

Penny, the family dog, was small to medium in size. His coat was black with a white bib beneath his chin. He had a fascination for the hand-cars, and he and the other dogs in the neighborhood chased after them, barking loudly, completely unaware that a leg could easily get caught between the wheel and track, severing the appendage.

She knew whenever the train whistle sounded her mother would call for her to come inside for lunch. In their case, it was called dinner. Their three meals each day consisted of breakfast, dinner, and supper. Her siblings were all at school, and through the day it was just she and her mother. Her father was at work in the coal mine. Each afternoon she watched and waited for him, and when he appeared in the alley, he was covered with coal dust as he carried his lunch bucket. He always wore his pit cap with the carbide lamp attached at the very top of the cap. The carbide lamp burned brightly whenever a miner was working underground. She ran toward him, reaching out her hand to carry his lunch bucket the rest of the way home. At four years of age, she was the youngest of a large family. That young girl was me, and this is my story.

ONE

Trains and Hobo Jungles

I GREW UP the youngest of twelve children. Well, that number does not include the two who died in infancy, but that still classifies me as the youngest. My brother, Otho, was five years old when my mother and dad married, so he was actually the oldest. My dad's first wife died of tuberculosis, and although they had four children, only one child had survived, that being Otho. The deaths of the children were most likely due to their mother's ill health, taking place in the early 1920s when tuberculosis was very common. Together there were twelve living children. My dad often said they were cheaper by the dozen.

There was a baby girl born, younger than me, who lived only forty-five minutes. The last child was our brother, Richard, a preemie who died at two months. My mother's body was no doubt tired from having so many children, and in fact, she had also suffered several miscarriages. My mother was thirty-six when I was born. She looked much older than she actually was. As a child, she had suffered typhoid fever. There was a large span of years between the older children and the younger ones. By the time I was old enough to remember much, my three older brothers had left home, and two sisters soon followed. By today's standards, my sisters had married far too young, but I'm sure they dreamed of falling in love, getting married, and having their own homes and families, which would allow them to live their "happily ever after."

I was born at home on Mother's Day, May 13, 1945. In most cases, if our mother did not have a midwife to help with the delivery, my dad assisted. He was experienced, having helped with several of our mother's deliveries. Unless there was a problem, the doctor was called only when the birth was near, and then only to make sure both the mother and the baby were both doing well. At the arrival of the doctor, he checked the mother, signed the birth certificate, weighed and named the baby, and gave mom instructions on postpartum care. By now, I'm sure she was quite skilled in that sort of thing, so it was plain and simple, over and done quickly.

On the day I was born, my parents had not selected a name. After announcing the gender, and trying to choose a name, our dad asked if anyone wanted to name me. My brother Charles was sitting on the sofa in the living room while reading a comic book. When he heard my dad ask the question, he called out the name of the girl featured in the comic book to our parents. And so it was, because my dad who was hoping for a boy, decided to call me Bobbi.

Until I was about four years old, we lived in a house where the railroad tracks were so close to our front door, the vibrations from the train shook the house, or at least they rattled the windows. We became accustomed to the train whistles. Growing up, it seems we always lived next to the railroad tracks. We lived in two different houses where an overpass was nearby, and where the trains passed over Emerson Street. Underneath the overpass were girders with enough space in which to fit our family. Many times during a storm, our dad would take our mom and the family to the overpass to wait for the storm to subside. There were only two things that I knew for certain of which my dad was afraid: The first was a storm, and the second was a mouse.

Tom Socks was our cat, and any time he caught a mouse, he hid it in one of my dad's work boots. My dad became livid, threatening the life of the cat, and then he calmed down only as my siblings rescued the cat. One afternoon, my sisters came home with four white mice that someone at school had given them. It did not take long for our dad to insist that they return the mice to their rightful owner immediately, because they certainly would not be taking up residency in his house.

We had a radio which stood upright on the floor. It was actually taller than me. My folks liked to listen to *The Grand Ole Opry* on Saturday nights. One of the country singers was Little Jimmy Dickens, and I had heard stories that he was quite short. I was told that in order to sing, he had to stand on a wooden box to reach the microphone. As I listened to him sing, I imagined him standing on a box, and I thought he was somewhere inside our radio. I often looked behind our radio, and as I saw the glass tubes lit up, I believed this was the actual studio where the singing took place.

We soon moved again, and yes, the train tracks were still close to the house, however, a little farther away from the house than where we had previously lived. There was no overpass nearby. Each spring, there was a parade of hobos jumping from the empty boxcars located toward the far rear of the freight train. It was in these freight cars that supplies such as grains were loaded, ready for delivery at various railroad stations. I know the men must have been hungry, because they went door-to-door asking for food almost immediately after clearing out of the cars. They vacated the boxcars before the train reached its destination and pull into the Railroad Yards, home of the Wabash Railroad in Moberly Missouri. My mother never failed to give them something to eat, and they retreated to a wooded area on the other side of the tracks. She knew what it was like to be hungry and to do without food, having experienced this herself.

Some of the neighborhood kids told stories that there was a "Hobo Jungle" nearby, and I was led to believe that in the spring before the transients arrived, a group of kids would sneak away to go investigate. They told me how they stayed there pretending to be hobos before returning home. I never knew if this was some kind of story they concocted to try and scare me or not. My mother seemed to think that this was just some kind of malarkey. That's the word she used.

As far as I know, these men never caused mischief, but never the less, we were instructed by our parents to stay away from the area the others were talking about. My dad wasn't sure exactly where the transients did stay, but evidently the men remained at some location, going about our town to find odd jobs. Quite often, residents would purposely save up jobs and repairs until spring, knowing that the transients would come. To be able to purchase food, the men worked for reasonable wages, making it a bargain for both sides. When the weather began to turn cold, they rode the rails back to the warmer climates avoiding the harsh Missouri winters.

It was in this same town and along these same tracks, that upon returning from WWII, soldiers threw hands full of coins out of the windows of the passenger cars in which they were riding. I was born earlier in May that same year. My older siblings would stand at a distance from the tracks, waving and cheering to the soldiers. As soon as the train was out of sight, the children scurried to the areas where the money had been scattered. They quarried through the gravel, collecting the treasure.

The Wabash Railroad in Moberly employed a great many of the local men. The railroad tracks ran through the northern part of the downtown area and into the railroad yard, and the Round House, where the switching of the railroad cars took place, as well as the unloading of freight. There was a depot, so those arriving could meet someone picking them up. Tickets could also be purchased for departure, and the ticket holder could wait there ready to embark. I envied the children of men who were employed by the railroad. They could ride the train anywhere within the state for free. I had been told they took trips to Kansas City or Saint Louis, or even for just a day of shopping. I was never on a train until 1962 when I was seventeen, and that was to go visit my sister in the Kansas City area. The cost of a one-way ticket was four dollars and fifty-five cents.

Before I was old enough to attend school, I watched my mother as she bustled around the house, cooking, cleaning, and washing clothes on a scrub board. Most of the time she was either singing or humming. Sometimes she would ever-so-softly whistle, "Blessed Assurance," the hymn written by Fannie Crosby. It was always the same song. It became one of my favorites. This song would end up being very relative to my life. She assigned me small tasks, but I mostly remember that she gave me the Sears and Roebuck catalog, and I would cut out pictures to use for paper dolls. The remainder of the catalog was placed in the outhouse. I had always hoped for the stand-up cardboard dolls at the five and dime, but the catalog dolls had to do, because we couldn't afford the others. I would lay on the floor pressing my face against the coolness of the linoleum floor. Many times I fell asleep and napped where I had been playing. My mother would just let me sleep. The flowers on the linoleum were worn and faded because my mom scrubbed it daily. She always said it wasn't a sin to be poor, but it was wrong to be dirty.

Each afternoon I waited patiently for my siblings to arrive home from school hoping that at least one of them would play with me. There was no one close to my age in the neighborhood except a young boy named Billy, who lived just a few houses down from us. The days were pretty long without my siblings. One day my mother allowed me to go play with Billy. She watched as I went, and when it was time for me to come home, she stood outside and called for me. Billy and I had been sitting on the edge of their porch looking through Little Golden Books. I was fascinated with one book in particular, *Three Little Kittens*. I knew that it was wrong to take something that didn't belong to me, but I wanted that book so badly.

The next day, my mother caught me reading this same book. She asked me where I had gotten the book, and I shrugged my shoulders as if to say I didn't know. Without saying a word, my mother took me by my hand and led me back to Billy's house, insisting that I return the book to its rightful owner and apologize for stealing the book. How in the world did she know? I began sobbing, and while still sobbing, I managed to say, "I'm sorry," and through my very emotional tears, I vowed to never do something like this ever again. She did not spank me, but forcing me to confront my wrongdoing was punishment enough.

This was close to the time that we had gotten our first phone. Our dad needed it for work, because he was delivering coal to customers. When they called, our mother took the order from the customer. The phone hung on the wall, and I could not reach it. We were on a party line, so one neighbor could listen to another's conversation. My sisters were in great trouble for using it to call local grocery stores and ask if they had Prince Albert in a can. If they answered, "Yes," the sister making the call would say, "You better let him out before he smothers." They also called other numbers to ask if their refrigerator was running. They didn't care which number they called. Again, if the answer was "Yes," they would say, "You better go catch it because it just ran past my house." These pranks soon came to an abrupt halt when our mother caught them.

I recall a horrible thunderstorm. I was horrified of the storms and to drown out the loud thunder, I placed my hands over my ears. I was even more afraid of the lightening that followed each clap of thunder. Sometimes it just seemed to bounce off the ground. It was during one of those horrible storms that our dad stepped to the kitchen door. He was holding the screen door when everything happened so quickly. We heard the enormous sound, and then we saw the flash. Our dad was knocked back into the dining room and fell to the floor. He had been struck by the bolt of lightning. The firemen arrived and took him to the McCormick Hospital. Upon careful examination, everything seemed to be fine, but an odd thing had happened. Our dad had, years before, been diagnosed with a leaky heart valve, but now the doctor said that he could not detect even the slightest of a murmur. Although lightning strikes claim many victims each year, why on earth did this happen? For years, we wondered about this, and just how this could have occurred. Was this the very thing that had closed the leaky heart valve? We would never know for sure, but God knew.

At the age of six, I began my first year of elementary school. There was a kindergarten, but since it was not free, I could not attend. I was very shy and introverted. I was one of the smallest children in my class. My first grade teacher's name was Mrs. Thomas, and I thought she was beautiful. She had pretty hair, and she always smelled so nice. The Principal's name was Mrs. Patrick, and she was older, had dark hair, and was tall and thin. I think she must have known how shy I was, because whenever she would visit our class, she would often pick me up and set me in the sandbox, which stood elevated off the floor. She would squeeze me gently, or pat my head until I smiled back. She also knew that I had older siblings in other classes.

I recall a small pond just a short distance from our house. It was on the opposite side of the tracks, next to Orscheln Motors. During the winter, the pond would always freeze over, and some of my older siblings would take our mother's galvanized washtub, and they would take turns climbing into it as one of the other siblings would spin them out over the surface of the frozen pond. The tub would swirl until it reached a stopping point on the other side. Looking back, we can now see how dangerous this must have been, because the pond also contained debris that had been dumped into the pond, which became frozen beneath the surface. Of course we didn't know this at that time. Our mother could not keep an eye on us every minute of the day, so she assumed that we were playing safely. In those days, danger was not lurking around every corner like it is today. I have often wondered about the many times God must have protected us.

It was around the edges of this very pond that my sisters searched for crawdads. They took them home, cut the tails off and fried the tails. They had heard this was a delicacy, so they fried them and tasted them to see. I don't recall ever wanting to taste any of their experimental dishes.

Huey, Dewey and Louie were cartoon duck characters created in the 1930s for Walt Disney Productions. They were also the names of three ducks owned by our twin sisters. These ducks on the other hand, were of a wild species and lived in a cage elevated up and off the ground. The cages were to keep them from falling victim to a predator. They had been given to both girls by the father of a friend. We spent many hours gently removing them from their cage, allowing them to peck in the dirt for bugs and worms. After a period of time, we returned them to their cage. One day the ducks disappeared, never to be seen again. They never knew who or what the perpetrator was, but so much for Huey, Dewey, and Louie, our wild ducks.

When I was small, I was very shy, my feelings were easily hurt. When I cried, I rubbed my eyes with clinched fists, which caused my eyes to redden. My dad called me his little pink-eyed rabbit, and my brother called me a weasel. I was adept at finding ways to entertain myself, and I was quite content to do so. Before ever attending school, I had learned many of the basics. We did not have a public kindergarten, but as my mother and sisters worked with me, by age three I could recite my ABCs, along with my numbers. I could also spell my name, and by age four I could write my name. By age eight, I could recite the Preamble to the U.S. Constitution.

As we walked back and forth to school, my sisters were protective of me, always holding my hand. I loved to read books and I liked to play school with the sock dolls my mother made for me. I taught them everything I had learned, which meant reading "Dick and Jane" books to them. I was the teacher, and they my students. I did not participate in sports, because I had an extreme iron deficiency and running made me tired. My parents made me take an iron tonic from the Rexall Drug Store. It was supposed to increase my appetite, but I would not take it unless my dad took it as well. The tonic did increase both our appetites, and between the two of us, we could consume a lot of food. Not only could I not run, I could not hit the ball. I had a depth perception problem which still plagues me to this very day. I was always content to sit quietly and play with friends, play school, read a book, or mostly sing.

There was a Dairy Queen close to the school. The owner loved kids, and had an agreement with the students that anyone who brought him a paper from class, which had been graded with a perfect score, would receive a small chocolate or vanilla ice cream cone. He initialed the paper so that we could use it only once. Many of us enjoyed ice cream on a regular basis, which was definitely an incentive to every one of us.

There was also a donut shop in the same area of the Dairy Queen. We could smell the fresh donuts from a block away. They also had day old donuts, and we could buy a long-john for a penny. On some Saturday mornings, we walked to the donut shop to buy a brown bag full of day old glazed donuts for a quarter. In order to freshen them, our mother would heat the donuts in the oven for several minutes, and then she would allow me to dunk mine in coffee.

At school I made a number of friendships, and some of those friendships remained through high school. Before school each morning, we played together until we heard the school bell summoning everyone into their classroom. At recess, we waited for one another on the playground, and we played on the swings, see-saws, and merry-go-round. The girls grouped together unless she was a tomboy, and in that case, she would go with the boys and play ball.

I recall one specific day when I came home from school and I told my mother that my class was collecting food and clothing for the poor. Our teacher had asked us to bring the items the next day. I will never forget that occasion. My mother looked at me and said matter-of-factly, "Honey, we are the poor!" I could not believe what she was saying. I didn't realize we were poor, so those words stung my heart. It did not seem at all that way to me. I thought poor people had nothing. After all, we were such a large family, and we had so much fun. It was that day that I learned a valuable lesson. I learned that being poor isn't the end of the world, or something of which to be ashamed, or allow it to define you. The next morning, my mother handed me a paper bag. Tucked inside the bag was a can of peas, and a child's blouse. That was exactly who my mother was. She was very giving, and she had a heart of gold.

Many times when there was a school program, especially if there was music, I was given a part to play. For our school Christmas program a first-grade girl was needed to play the part of Suzy Snowflake. I was chosen, and I was to wear some sort of short white costume with lots of netting. It was to be decorated with strands of silver garland and glitter. I was taught to twirl around and sing, "Here comes Suzy Snowflake, dressed in a snow white gown. Tap, tap, tapping on the window pane to tell you she's in town. Here comes Suzy Snowflake soon you will hear her say 'Come out everyone and play with me, I haven't long to stay.'"

There was only one problem. My mother did not have the resources to make the costume. My sister Leota volunteered to make it, which was great because she also had a sewing machine. I had no idea that it would turn out to be so lovely. At that time, my sister lived 21 miles from Moberly, but she finished the costume, in time to bring it to my class for the final rehearsal. The Christmas program was wonderful, and I felt like a princess.

My dad frowned on anyone who encouraged us to believe in Santa Claus because we never received gifts. My dad told us that we would be disappointed, so he chose not to teach us to believe there was a Santa, an Easter Bunny or Tooth Fairy, because that would be lying. We also never received a birthday gift or have a cake. I think deep down inside, each of us hoped that there was at least a Santa. Every Christmas morning, we each received an apple, an orange, nuts, and some hard ribbon and pillow candy. These items were placed in our very own bowl on the kitchen table, from the oldest to the youngest. We always had a huge meal together, and I loved the red Jell-O. I laughed and said it shook like Santa's belly. Sometimes my mother sliced bananas in the Jell-O.

We could not afford to buy a Christmas tree, but each year one of our siblings asked their teacher if they could have the tree from their classroom. On the last day before Christmas break, the students in each class had a party with a gift exchange. At the end of the day, one of my siblings brought the tree home, along with the wrapping paper and ribbon that had been discarded from the party. We made red and green paper chains from construction paper, and we would always string popcorn to put on the tree. We gathered small empty boxes and wrapped them with the paper and ribbon that we brought home. We placed them under the tree to make it look like there were actually gifts. When we were finished, we stood back and admired our work, and afterward, we all sang Christmas carols.

According to my mother, there were times when the teachers at school asked if they could adopt us for Christmas. My dad was very proud, and declined, saying it was nobody's business, and he did not want charity. One Christmas during my second grade year, my mother accepted. I think perhaps a few years before this, a few teachers had also delivered presents, although our dad did not like it at that time either. She told my dad what she had done, and that the children deserved to have a good Christmas. I'm sure they argued, but she stood her ground. The gifts from the teachers were delivered, and were hidden somewhere out of sight. I could never quite figure out where they could have been hidden, because our house was small. Later, I thought perhaps they may have been in the attic. That particular Christmas I received a stuffed reindeer with a large red nose. I named the reindeer Rudy. This gift, however, was not to last long.

It was in January, 1952, which was my second year of school when our home burned to the ground. It was shortly after the same Christmas that I had received Rudy, My dad had awakened and had gone outside to use the outhouse. What happened next was catastrophic. On the way back to the house, he saw the flames. He ran inside, calling out to awaken everyone. A few months previously, my dad had purchased a car. He quickly backed it away from the house so that we could take shelter inside the car. It was then that our mother noticed that my twin sisters were missing. My dad had awakened them, but they had both gone back to sleep. My dad ran back inside the house to successfully rescue my sisters. We were all wearing our sleeping clothes and it was cold. Inside the car we waited for the firetruck as we watched the flames leaping from the roof, but there was nothing they could do to save a thing.

Before the firemen arrived, my dad remembered that he had placed some money from the sale of two hogs in the top drawer of the chest in their bedroom. He couldn't afford to lose the money. He crawled on his stomach through two rooms to try to retrieve it. He was overcome by smoke so the firemen used a noose-type hook around his ankle to pull him from the burning and smoke engulfed house. My sisters almost perished, my dad almost died from smoke inhalation, and my stuffed reindeer was now gone. I sobbed, because that was the first new toy I had ever received.

We were taken to a neighbor's house where they made

room for us until we could locate another place to stay. The public began donating clothing and furniture, because that's what small towns do. They come together in times of crisis. Within a few days it was decided that we would set up housekeeping in my older brother Charles' garage. Until that time came, our dad continued to drive us to our present school each morning. This was in January, and there was snow on the ground. The news spread throughout the school about what had happened to us. I remember wearing a white blouse that had been donated, and it had embroidered pink flowers on the collar. One of my classmates approached me and said, "You're wearing my blouse." I was shocked, knowing even at my young age, a lesson in mercy, and being kind to others. After we moved, I never saw this rude classmate again until we were in junior high, but I doubt that she even remembered the incident.

TWO

The Cadillac Hearse

MY BROTHER'S GARAGE was very large, and it was not attached to his house. Our parents and older siblings used two by four lumber to build a few separating walls, and they flattened large cardboard boxes and nailed them over the studs to create separate sleeping quarters apart from the living quarters. They said cardboard is a good insulator. My dad had gotten the boxes from a local company that manufactured caskets. They knew our dad, so they donated the boxes. We were also given large stand-up boxes to use as wardrobes in which to hang our clothing. The garage had once been an auto repair shop, but when my brother bought the house, he used the garage to sell fireworks for the Fourth of July each year.

There were a number of us sleeping in the same bed, but that was nothing new. Sometimes there were so many kids in the same bed, we had to sleep crossways. We used to say if another's foot was itching, and they reached down to scratch it, they would end up scratching the foot of someone else. Being the youngest, and smallest, I was usually the one who fell out of bed each night, or I was pushed out, and most often I found myself underneath the bed, awaiting the daylight to enter the room and drive out the darkness. That's what I learned in Sunday School. Darkness cannot drive out light, but light can drive out darkness. This became my greatest fear, and as a result, I slept with my head covered until I was thirteen years old.

After the fire and relocating to my brother's garage, we had to change schools. This time we would be going to Terrill School, which was a large red brick country school with one large room. We attended school with some of the Kennedy children. Our sister was dating one of the older Kennedy boys at that time. The school contained grades one through eight, and each class was set up in a certain section of the large room. The classes stretched out over the entire main floor of the building.

We had only one teacher, and her name was Mrs. Overfelt. She moved to each class with precision, and everyone did their work quietly. There was also a basement, and Mr. Overfelt also did the cooking. Her daughter, Elaine, was an eighth grade student, and she also helped prepare lunch. Sometimes we had sandwiches with vegetables, fruit, and cookies. We went to the basement to eat lunch, and I experienced putting ketchup in my beans for the first time, which became one of my favorite meals.

I was the only student in the second grade, so when Mrs. Overfelt saw that I could do third grade work, she asked for permission from the Moberly School District Superintendent to allow me to join in with the third grade class. My brother, Mick, was also in third grade. The Superintendent came to visit our school, and I was called to meet with him. He asked me many questions, and it was then that Mrs. Overfelt asked me if I would I recite the Preamble of the U.S. Constitution. I had learned some of the things the other classes were learning, because each day when I was finished with my classwork, I paid very close attention to what the other classes were being taught. It became easy for me to remember a large amount of what they were also learning. I was allowed to join the class, but that did not mean I was a third grade student.

Since we now lived outside the city limits, it was too far to walk. Our brother took us to school each morning. My dad traded our car for an older Cadillac hearse, and each day he picked us up from school. A few of us rode in the very back where there were two large doors that swung open. While seated on the floor, we felt we were rich because of all the wine color plush interior and carpeting. I had no idea what was the original purpose of the vehicle. I had never been to a funeral, so I just knew the hearse was massive and shiny, and it was not a pickup truck. I could lay down and the carpet felt amazing.

There were two African-American men who worked with my dad. Each morning he picked them up for work and took them back home after work in the afternoon. It was very early in the morning when my dad normally picked the men up, so it was still dark. They were close friends, but the next morning when he arrived to take them to work in the hearse, they refused to get in, saying they were not going to ride in a "dead man's wagon." As I recall that story, I have to chuckle at how my dad always retold it. He also told us these men were superstitious. They ended up riding with my dad, and they got used to the hearse, but our dad did remove the curtains.

There was a Polio epidemic during the year of 1952. There were many children affected by this epidemic, and some were left crippled. When we heard this news, we were very attentive. During that exact year, I had missed a month of school. I lay in bed, unable to walk, because my legs ached so badly, and I couldn't stand up on my own. My sisters brought my homework from school. My parents had no idea what was going on, and believed it was perhaps growing pains. In most cases, my parents did not seek medical attention if they could treat the condition themselves, and by the time we began hearing very much about this epidemic, I was already back at school.

Not being able to afford a doctor, my parents often turned to homeopathic treatment. My mother rubbed my legs with Absorbine Junior. The liquid was in a bottle, and was oily and greenish in color. It smelled like wintergreen and the bottle had a spongy roller top. I complained that her hands were rough, but being a child I had not considered the fact that she did the laundry on a scrub board, so I should not have complained. My dad also bought Bayer chewable orange-flavored baby aspirin for me, and my mother hid the bottle from the older kids. After a few weeks, and plenty of rest, she started getting me up and walking me around chairs that she placed in a circle. I held onto the backs of the chairs and with my mother's help, I was able to exercise. When I regained my leg strength, I returned to school.

The same peculiar thing happened during the summer of my fourth grade, and when it had passed, I seemed to be just fine. When I was grown with children of my own, I experienced another episode, unable to walk, was hospitalized and placed in traction. My orthopedic doctor informed me that I suffered from Spondylolisthesis from birth. This is a spinal disorder in which someone is born with an upper vertebra misaligned too far forward and formed onto the bone below it. This puts pressure on the bones in the lower back. He was reasonably sure that was what had happened both times during my childhood. It was no wonder that I could not run well, and now I knew the reason.

1954 was the year the Sabin Polio Vaccine was discovered and every child was encouraged to receive it. Because of my previous situation with walking, my parents thought it was a good idea for me to get the vaccine. My siblings and I went to the school auditorium to receive this vaccine. I didn't like needles, so I was surprised that when I reached the nurses, we were given a sugar cube to suck on. Instead of using a needle, the vaccine was placed on the cube and taken orally. There was still a second vaccine administered at a later date, and within a few years, it became injectable.

When we moved from my brother's house, and left Terrill School, we moved about six miles west of Moberly to the small town of Huntsville. Huntsville was the county seat of Randolph County. Our house was in the country, and it was surrounded by strip pits which were abandoned after the coal had been extracted from the land. There were large hills of dirt and shale, which at times left a stench in the air. When we were close to the strip pits, it smelled like rotten eggs. There were streams of water that trickled down the piles of rocky dirt and black shale, but it was also sulfur water from the excavated areas. The streams looked rusty. The streams flowed over the black shale that remained covering the ground. We waded in the streams anyway. We played on the piles of dirt, and we thought that it was so much fun.

The County Dump was just over and down the hill, and it became our retreat. It was just about as much fun as a shopping mall, but it didn't smell nearly as good. We hid and watched, and whenever we saw a big truck unload and leave the dumpsite, and when we were sure that no one was looking, especially our mom, we would head over the hill to see the treasures that the trucks had left behind. When the Bell System switched from the crank-type telephones, we found an abundance of the old phones discarded. They were the beautiful wooden wall phones. We loaded our wagon and pulled it back up the hill to our playhouse. We played with the phones, not realizing how valuable they would one day be. We also found a supply of waffle irons, so we opened a café in our playhouse. When we moved from Huntsville, we had to leave those items behind, in our playhouse.

We found a few boards and five gallon buckets, and we brought all of these home with us and used them to set up benches so that we could play church and school in the strip pits. We positioned a bucket at each end, and placed the boards over them, creating benches. We sang the hymns that our mother had taught us, and the older kids took turns playing preacher, convincing me that I was doomed to burn in Hell. When our dad found out how frightened his baby girl was, and the reason why I was crying, they were all punished.

One day we went down over the hill to investigate recently dumped items, and as we left to go home, we noticed that Mick was not with us. We thought he might be ahead of us, but a few minutes later, we saw him coming over the hill and he was holding something bright red. One of my sisters said, "Oh look, Mick has found some bright red ribbon."

It certainly was not ribbon. It was quite evident by his clothing, and the fact that he was holding one of his wrists with his opposite hand, that he had gotten into some broken glass, and had seriously cut his wrist, severing the small artery, and slightly damaging a tendon. Our dad arrived home simultaneously, and applying pressure, he wrapped Mick's wrist in a towel. He drove to the hospital in Moberly where he received stitches in his wrist. Each of us was given strict instructions from that day forward, to stay away from the dump. We did, well, almost.

The house we rented had red siding, and I asked if it was a barn. There were no close neighbors except the Wolverton family, and we lived on a gravel road. We walked to school, and it was not bad walking to school, because we walked downhill. The problem was the enormous hill going back home. Every day walking back up the hill made my side ache. I stopped and spat on a rock and replaced the rock exactly as I had found it. This was an old wives' tale meant to cure an ache in a person's side. My siblings sometimes felt sorry for me, and took turns giving me a piggy-back ride. At this time I was still pretty small, however I overcame this as I got older.

The red house had a huge porch extending from the front, leaving the porch a great distance off the ground. During the hot nights, we made a pallet on the floor of the porch and slept outside. We laid there on our blankets, and we looked at the brilliance of the stars, and listened to the night sounds from the birds, frogs and the crickets. We weren't afraid of wolves or wild animals, because we did not think they would be able to climb high enough to reach the porch. The older kids told stories, mostly ghost stories, and most of the time, I drifted off to sleep before the stories were ever finished.

Mick pestered us in any way that he could. As an example, he intentionally kept one of his toenails longer that the others. After we were in bed at night, he would drag the longer toenail on the floor, creating a sound like chalk on a chalkboard. This drove us berserk. My sisters also bribed him to sit in a chair while they practiced pin-curling his hair. His hair was thick and dark, and when they finished brushing it, he looked like Curly of the Three Stooges.

There was a huge tree just beyond the porch. My siblings found a large rope, and using a ladder, they tied the rope to the tree, using it to swing off the porch and out to the tree. Then they pushed out from the tree with their feet, and returned to the porch, Tarzan style. They left the rope secured to the porch for easy access. Our dad found it and those who were found guilty were lectured. He did, however allow them to build a rope swing from a limb with a rope and board seat.

Up and over the hill from the back of our house was a cemetery, which scared me to death. If, for some reason I was the only child left at home during the day, I did not dare venture outside to play. I remained inside the house making sure to stay close to my mother.

We had a dirt cellar beneath the house. Our mother stored our vegetables and canned goods in the cellar because it was cool. It was also a safe-haven for our dad's home brew. Our mother had a large stone crock in which she would make sauerkraut. When she was finished canning the sauerkraut, our dad gathered his supplies and used the crock to prepare for the distillation process.

Daddy used the necessary items, including brewer's yeast. He had a good supply of brown glass beer bottles, and a bottle capper. The capper sealed the lid on a bottle as the handle was pressed, which also squeezed the lid to make it tight. For a nickel, he convinced us to wash the bottles for him by sterilizing them in a galvanized tub of hot water. There was a small fire under the tub which was used to heat the water. He funneled the brew into the bottle and used the bottle capper to seal them. He took them to the cellar and placed them on the shelves to await a specific time for them to complete the fermenting process. When it was time, he sat underneath a shade tree and drank his home brew.

The amusing part of this, was that our mother was a teetotaler, despising alcohol in any form. She devised a scheme that was quite brilliant. When our dad was gone, our mother would sneak down to the cellar, and ever-so-gently loosen some of the caps. Hours later, the lids would begin popping off the bottles. Our dad would hear them, utter a curse word, scratch his head and wonder why some of the bottles did not seal. Our mother just grinned slightly as she turned and walked away. We knew what she had done, but the secret was safe with us. We did not like his drinking any more than she liked it.

This was the same cellar that our mother once used to scare the stuffing out of us. It was close to being dark, and we had company. We were down near the strip pits playing church or something, and we heard a commotion.

We looked up toward the house, only to see a white figure coming out of the underground cellar beneath the house. Whatever it was, we did not know. The figure was wearing a long white cape, and it was howling. We fled our meeting so fast, that it's a wonder we didn't trip over one another.

Gasping for breath, we burst through the back door into the kitchen only to see our mother standing at the kitchen stove. It was many years before she confessed it was she who had thrown a bed sheet over her head and gone to the cellar hoping to play a joke on us. I never could figure out how she beat us to the house. Our mother was a person who liked to play jokes on her children, and then she laughed at us for falling for the joke. She was more fun when our dad was not at home, becoming much more serious when he was there. I think she was just a kid at heart. Our friends loved her humor.

We loved to go berry picking, and there were plenty of blackberry bushes along the roadside. This coincided at the same time during the summer when we attended Bible School. We attended Bible School in the morning, and went berry picking in the afternoon. I always wore sleeves because I didn't like getting stuck by thorns. The size of the pan that our mother used for a cobbler required a lot of berries. It was a huge blue granite pan. We picked in pairs, so it did not really take that long to find enough berries for the cobbler. My older sister, Doris, was usually my partner, but I ate more than I picked. We took our bucket home, cleaned and washed the berries, and that night our mother served us the most delicious blackberry cobbler. I liked the crust, and I still prefer cobbler over pie because cobbler has more juice.

In the fall of the following year, our dad announced that

we were moving back to Moberly. He had plans to open another coal mine. We moved in October. I remember the specific season, because the leaves were changing colors and drifting to the ground. When we arrived on Collins Avenue, the house in which we would be living stood on the corner and it had a large front porch. It had brown siding that looked like brick, however it was asphalt rolled siding. There was a huge tree at the very corner, and a large lot in between our house and the nearest neighbor. Later we played ball in this empty lot. There was a wooded area to the east that became a great place to play. There was a large shed at the very back of the lot, with enough space for our dad to park his truck. It would be in this house that we would make many lasting memories. There was an alley that separated the houses on Collins and Hinton Avenues. Mr. and Mrs. Courier lived directly behind us on the opposite side of the alley facing Hinton.

Since our dad could not stand a messy yard, to the younger kids he immediately assigned the job of raking the leaves. We took breaks from raking to bury ourselves in the leaves. There was a ditch next to the road that ran along the front of our house, and into this ditch we were told to rake the leaves. Our dad came outside to set them afire. The older kids took care of the burning leaves. This would be an almost daily job until the tree was bare, and often the neighborhood kids joined in to help. Dad didn't mind that we played in the leaves, but he expected us to rake them up when we were finished. To me, the smell of burning leaves was wonderful. I still become a little bit nostalgic by that smell. As we burned the leaves, I had flashbacks about the stories I had read in my earlier years in the "Dick and Jane" books, and I could almost see Mr. Zeke, their neighbor, raking and burning leaves.

We never owned a home at this time, so we lived in rented houses on the poorer side of town. There were plenty of other families who were in the same situation, and certainly plenty of kids. We felt like one big happy family. In fact, one evening when my dad was ordering all of us to go inside and get ready for bed, he included one of the neighbor boys. The boy simply said, "But Mr. Skinner, I don't live here."

In reply, my dad just shrugged and said, "Huh," turned away, and walked toward the house.

We enrolled in West Park Elementary School. The elementary schools in Moberly were divided by different sections of town with a school in each section, plus a school in the center. There was North Park, South Park, West Park, and East Park, and the school geared toward the middle was Central. Lincoln was a separate school for black students. During 1956, and during my fifth grade, our school system became integrated. Through the next few years, Lincoln School was converted into a school for all seventh grade students to attend. In addition, there was a Catholic school for students through a certain grade. Moberly Junior High contained grades nine and ten, which was the freshmen and sophomore classes. The juniors and seniors attended classes at the two-year junior college.

Each day we played outside with the neighborhood kids, and on weekends, we came home only for lunch, and then back outside again. We played ball in the street, and at dusk all the grownups sat on their porches and talked, while the kids played Hide and Seek, Red Rover, Rotten Egg, and

Blind Man's Bluff. We played in the rain, waded in the ditches filled with rain water, captured crawdads, caught lightening bugs, and went barefoot. We pinched off the glowing part of the lightening bug and wore it as a ring. Doing that now, sounds disgusting.

Our parents did not have to worry about us, and we always stuck together. Looking down our street, there was a row of houses on either side. The adults living in the houses always kept a close eye on the children. If they saw a problem, they would report it to the parents, and the parents knew for sure that the neighbor was right, taking their word for it. At dusk, we were called to come in, and my dad insisted we go to bed. We hated having to go to bed when it was not yet dark, but our dad got up very early each morning for work. My mother always insisted that our feet be clean before we climbed into bed. That was always strange to me, and I couldn't figure out why she didn't mention the other parts of our body, but even though we were poor our mother still said it was wrong to be dirty.

In order to feel a breeze, we slept with the doors to our house open with only a small hook latch for the screen door. During the day our house became full of flies from all of the kids running in and out, fanning the doors. Our mother hated flies, and she would hand us towels, and make us begin in the back bedrooms and "shoo" flies from the back rooms to the front of the house. One of my siblings would stand at the front door and open it for the flies to escape. That lasted for a few hours, and then we had to repeat the process over again.

The only inside plumbing we had was in the kitchen, which was a single water pipe for cold water. We warmed our water on the stove, and we had a galvanized bucket with water and a metal dipper to drink. We all drank from the same dipper, and no one contracted a disease, or died from doing so. We used an outhouse as a pit latrine, with a single hole, and traipsing down the path in cold weather was an unpleasant chore. I once picked up a Blacksnake laying on the path, thinking it was a piece of black rubber hose. I remember it was cold and clammy. After realizing what it was, I quickly threw it down, screamed, and ran back to the house. I am sure after that experience, I no longer needed to go. It was a few days before I felt willing to go to the privy alone.

We bathed in a galvanized tub, and during the warm months we placed the tub of water in the sun so it would be heated when we carried it inside. Using the coal stove in the kitchen would heat up the entire house, so warming the water in the sun was better. It must have been difficult for our mother to cook three meals a day on a coal stove or wood stove, especially during the hot summer months. We bathed in the kitchen, and hung a blanket up at the doorway for privacy. We didn't have doors to separate the rooms. The bathing began with the oldest to the youngest, and this did not occur every day. Sometimes the bath days were two days in a row for two separate groups. Being the youngest, I could always count on being the last one to bathe. My dad however, took a bath every day through the week. He was covered in coal dust when he came home from work, and there was no way my mom would allow the dust to be brought into her house. The bathing took place as soon as he walked through the door, where she would have everything ready; the water, soap, washcloth, and towel. The water was almost black when we carried it out near the shed to dump it out of the tub.

Down the street and around the corner, lived the Gravitt family. The dad's name was George and the mother was Edna. We identified with this family, as they had a number of children as well. The oldest to youngest was Franklin, Billy, Henry, Edna, Lavella, Hazel, and Rosie. Oh, what fun we had with that family.

Around that time, we had a pickup truck but it was used for my dad's work. He delivered coal to customers by which to heat their homes. Coal was a main source of fuel around Moberly for those not having gas. There were a number of coal mines. Many families had coal stoves or furnaces. Many businesses also had coal furnaces, as did the schools. It was the job of the school janitor to keep the furnaces stoked and burning, and in turn the heat would generate the steam for the radiators to heat each of the rooms.

The Gravitt family had no vehicle, but they did have a single horse-drawn wagon. George always hitched up his horse, known to us as Ted. As he drove the wagon down the street, the wagon seemed to glide smoothly, as Ted's clomping hooves struck the pavement in a precise rhythm. George took very good care of his horse and kept him well groomed. The horse was adorned by a brilliant harness, and the wagon was green. There was a wagon seat at the very front. The rest of the family sat in the back of the wagon. George often stopped in front of our house to talk with my dad. He would allow us to smooth Ted's silky horse hair, but he insisted that we stand in a particular spot so as to not scare him.

The Gravitt family went to town each Friday night by horse and wagon when the weather was decent. They were not the only family in town or the outskirts to travel by horse and wagon, because there were many others. The family had supper together at a local restaurant and they did their shopping. I was a bit jealous that they were able to do this, because we never did anything exciting like that. We were especially close to this family. All of the kids played together, and there was always something we could do together to stay entertained. My brother Mick ran around with Henry, but I don't care to think about the amount of mischief in which those two may have been involved. I preferred to hang out with Hazel and Lavella, who were closer in age to me.

Bobbi Smith

THREE

Hot Weather and Out-of-Town Company

DURING THE WARMER months, the ice delivery truck drove through the neighborhoods. The Moberly Ice House was a locally owned business in town that froze and sold blocks of ice to the public, but it was much easier to buy it from the ice man. We didn't have a refrigerator, but we had a wooden icebox on our enclosed back porch, and we used it to store food that might spoil. During the winter, we had a wooden box attached to the house just outside the kitchen window. We stored our cold food items inside the wooden box which acted as a cooler. We simply raised and lowered the window to gain access to the cold items. My dad lined the box with insulation so none of the items would freeze.

The hot months were here to stay for a while, so we kept a watchful eye out for the ice man. He drove a short black truck with doors that swung open at the rear where the blocks of ice were stored. We purchased the ice, and the delivery man carried the chunk of ice to the back porch, and using large tongs to handle the ice, he set it in the icebox. We never knew his name, so we just called him the "Ice Man." Meanwhile, back at his truck, the kids all gathered at the rear of his truck, and using a sharp pointed icepick to break into a block of ice, he handed a chunk to each of us standing in expectation. As he handed the ice to us, we quickly took it, and wrapped it in a piece of newspaper to keep it from melting, and also to protect our hand from the cold. We made the ice last as long as we possibly could without it melting. We licked the ice until our tongues felt like they were frozen, as the melted water ran down our arms. On a really hot day, this was a simple pleasure.

The summer of 1954 was one of the hottest summers on record in Missouri. I was nine years old. It was said that the temperatures reached close to 118 degrees. I don't know how true that is, but I can certainly remember how hot the nights were as we tried to fall asleep. Only the wealthy had air conditioning. We had a fan that our dad made from an old washing machine motor, and he reversed it in a window to draw a breeze into the house through the other windows. It may have helped a little, but the nights never cooled down to be considered very comfortable. When he and my older brother first made the fan, he tried placing it in the window without reversing it, and it blew the dishes off our mother's table.

Our neighbor had a water cooler in his window. I never actually knew how that worked. My dad called it a "contraption." I didn't know what a contraption was either. The previous year was labeled a drought, and with this year came the heat. From mid-June to mid-July, statistics say there were 137 heat related deaths across the state.

The extreme heat was responsible for such things as twisted railroads tracks caused by expanding rails in Kansas, as well as over 50 instances of streets buckling from the heat. I had read of those instances, and heard my dad talking about them. Water shortage problems were common throughout Kansas and Missouri. Young trees and plants with shallow root systems were very much in danger from the burning sun. Trees lost their leaves as they shriveled in the heat. Livestock died because the grass went dormant and ponds dried up. Since there was very little hay from the previous year because of the drought, farmers began selling their cattle at market.

It was reported that the extreme heat caused a Kansas City weather beacon to malfunction and forecast snow. I told my dad I bet that was a real shocker, and why would that happen? My dad explained that a weather beacon is usually on the roof of a tall building in the business district, but some are attached to a tower, which shows the local weather forecast in a code of colored or flashing lights. He also told me that I sure did ask a lot of questions, to which I usually responded, "How am I supposed to learn, if I don't ask questions?"

Once in a while our Uncle Lavern came to visit us. This was such a year for his periodic visit. He hopped a freight car and rode to Missouri. I think he must have been sorry he came because of the heat. He was what I would today call a "couch surfer." He was our mother's younger brother, and he spent most of the time with relatives in the Jeffersonville, Indiana area close to Kentucky. He looked a lot like his father, my Grandpa Charley. Since I never met my Grandpa Charley, but had only seen pictures of him, that meant that I also resembled my uncle, especially my hair and my eyes. He came for a visit every few years during the summer months. My dad called him a bum.

Uncle Lavern didn't have a job, but that man could really sing. He had his own guitar, which he brought with him. He had a voice that would speak to your heart, and he sounded exactly like Hank Snow, a country music singer of that day. He had just enough of the nasal sound to make it difficult to determine if it was Hank singing, or my uncle. Uncle Lavern also had a taste for beer.

My mother had warned Uncle Lavern to never come to her house when he was drinking. Taking his guitar and going to a downtown tavern, or as we called them, "beer joints," he told them his name was Justin Tubb, and that he was from Nashville. He would begin to play and sing, and his voice sounded so authentic that the men would buy him beer, and give him money. He knew when he had his limit of beer because of our mother's warning, so he would leave, having met some of the tavern's finest customers.

I loved my Uncle Lavern, and I was so attentive to his smoking needs to the point of taking my very last nickel and going to the neighborhood grocery store to buy smoking tobacco for him. He never refuse it. He smoked Bull Durham tobacco and it would come in a small cloth bag with a drawstring at the top. There was a package of cigarette papers attached, which were used to roll the cigarettes. My dad also rolled his own cigarettes, so I was familiar with the method. In my dad's case, he used Prince Albert in a can, and OCB papers, which he carried in the pocket of his bibbed overalls.

As we sat under a shade tree, I watched my uncle roll his first cigarette, grin, wink at me, and say, "Well Honey,

Uncle Lavern sure does appreciate this." I knew that first puff satisfied his craving for tobacco, so I would smile and feel pretty proud of myself for sacrificing my last nickel to make him happy. Maybe he would sing me a song. After a few weeks, his feet began to get the itch to move on, and he would hop into the boxcar of another train, and head out of town. We never knew where he was headed, or when we might see him again, but I was always sad to see him leave. My dad called him a gypsy.

Our mother took us to pick wild greens. When Uncle Lavern was visiting he also went along with us. We took a bushel basket with us in which to carry the greens. Our mother taught us the names of the greens, and we all became familiar with the various kinds. They were Dandelion, Sour Dock, Poke, Lamb's Quarter, Wild Mustard, and Sorrell. The mixture of these greens added a nice variety to our diet. She taught us the right mixture, and assured us she only wanted young Poke, because if it grew too large, it would become bitter. With all of us picking, it didn't take long to fill the basket. I was always amazed that after picking an entire basket, taking them home and washing them, cooking them and frying them down in bacon drippings, they only produced one large bowl full of the spinach-type food. I always poured a little apple cider vinegar on mine.

I came from a very large family on both my mother and father's side. We became very excited when we had out-of-town visitors. Occasionally the Potter family came for a visit. They were our cousins who lived in Kirksville, Missouri, and later moved to Wyoming. The Potters are my mother's side of the family. Their daughter and son-in-law had a camper in which they would stay. Many of the kids were the same ages as most of us, which made us happy. We referred to their parents as Aunt Onie and Uncle Pete, but actually Onie was our mother's cousin, and her real name was Iona. The younger kids would run and play, and the older ones entertained one another. We loved them so much, and after Uncle Pete accepted Jesus into his life, it changed the entire nature of the family.

Every few years the Parker family would also come for a random visit. My mother never looked pleased when they came. I think it was because many of them drank alcohol, or so I was told. They were an additional family of cousins, from Indiana, and again there were a number of kids. They were sort of related to both our mother, and our dad. My mother's sister was married to my dad's late wife's brother. As a child, I never could quite figure that one out.

Once the Parkers came for a visit during the Fourth of July. Their parents gave them money to purchase fireworks, which resulted in a constant blasting all day long. There was also a lot of eating and celebrating. Having fireworks was rare for us unless one of my siblings had extra money. I didn't like fireworks, because our dog Blackie, hid in the shed to escape the noise. I stayed close to him, because firecrackers scared me as well.

Once in a while during the summer months, our dad asked us to sweep the coal dust from the truck bed. We knew he was planning something, so after sweeping it, we carried buckets of water to also wash it out. We felt that he must be taking us somewhere. He was still operating the mine, but he wasn't delivering as much coal. During the summer he added to the stockpile of coal at the mine, in preparation for the next season of heating. Our method of cleaning the truck bed was to pour the water from the buckets and then sweep it out with a straw broom.

When the evening came, and we saw our mom coming out of the house, our dad would tell us to get into the truck and we would go for a ride. Of course we all had to either sit down, or stand up in the bed. While in town, he would insist that we sit down, but when we reached the country we could stand up and hold on tightly. If my older sisters saw someone they knew, they quickly hid so that no one would notice them. If this happened, Mick and I would start yelling and pointing to them to let their friends know they were with us.

In most cases, our dad drove us to an exclusive area with fancy homes just at the outskirts of town. There were rolling hills and grassy lawns, and the homes were so beautiful that we were simply awestruck. We were almost breathless from their beauty as we drove past them. We made guesses as to who owned the homes, and we thought the owners might be doctors or lawyers. We called it "Rich Man's Hill," and we would say, "When I grow up, I want to live in this house." We could feel the breeze in our faces and in our hair as we went up and down the hills. That was a time of pure joy. At that moment, we didn't care if people thought we were hillbillies or not. The wind felt amazing. It was worth the ride, and we were content.

I recall attending prayer meetings and revivals at a small Pentecostal church just around the corner from where we lived. It was located between our house, and where the Gravitt family lived. The church services were held in a large open room at the end of the house where Mr. and Mrs. Jordan lived. Sister Jordan was a woman preacher. She would preach "Hell-fire and damnation," and scare me to death. I don't know why everyone enjoyed scaring me. We sang to the top of our lungs, and she would ask if any of us wanted to share a testimony or sing. Of course I wanted to sing! I remember Edna Gravitt standing there, rocking back and forth as she prayed her heart out, and as George and Edna would share their testimonies. Edna always chewed gum, but she always wore a smile. The praying was in unison, and of one accord, so it could get pretty loud as we watched the Holy Spirit pour out. I just stood and watched in wonder. One day I would understand. Many years later I would identify as being "Bapticostal."

I was always anxious to go to Sunday School, but we didn't go to the same Pentecostal church, because they didn't have Sunday School. We went to the Baptist church and when I went to church, I could wear my best dresses, and my sisters helped me get ready and brushed my hair. I liked the way my hard soled shoes clicked on the floors inside the church. I liked the flannel board in my classroom, and I was amazed that the Bible characters would stick to the flannel as my teacher told us a Bible story. I was allowed to take my paperwork home, and I looked at it throughout the week as I tried to retell the story to my mother. I attended school with some of the same kids who also attended this church.

We wore hand-me-downs, and didn't really mind. Each school year the girls would each get one pair of shoes, socks, underwear, and two new dresses. My brother, Mick got a pair of shoes, two new shirts, and two pairs of jeans, socks and underwear. We wore a dress two days, and the other one for three days, alternating the dresses every week. We were expected to take care of the clothing and the shoes, and we were expected to change out of them into older ones when we got home from school. We also had one pair of shoes that we wore for good, and that was mostly to church on Sunday. My shoes were usually black patent leather, and my sisters would shine them with Vaseline Petroleum Jelly until I could see my reflection in them. I think my mom bought them at the Salvation Army. They had an area in part of the church basemen that sold and gave away used clothing. It was called a clothes closet.

During the summer when we were at home, we usually went barefoot. I received many hand-me-downs from my sisters, but I was so scrawny that my mother had to remake the clothes in order for them to fit me. She did this by hand, because she never had a sewing machine. She sewed the fabric together with tiny, tiny stitches. I watched her and I was fascinated. Sometimes she created her own patterns out of newspaper. When I grew up, I became a good seamstress like my mother, the only exception being, I was fortunate enough to have several types of machines. I'm not patient enough to sew tiny stitches.

When contagious childhood diseases were on the rise, whether it was measles, mumps, or chickenpox, parents tried to expose their children so that it could run its course throughout the family, and it would be over and done with and out of the way. If a child was suffering from mumps, the parents tried to keep the child as still as possible. Mumps can infect many parts of the body, but is best known for causing swelling of the salivary glands. To diagnose the disease, our mother felt our neck to determine if there was swelling of the glands. If she saw evidence of swelling, she would make us drink a spoonful of vinegar, or eat a sour pickle. As we swallowed the sour juices, or as we tried to talk or chew, it would become painful, and that's how she diagnosed us. One or both of the salivary glands became swollen, and sometimes one would swell a few days before the other.

If we had measles, we were made to stay in a darkened room. Headaches usually accompanied measles, and the less light, the better. They said it was hard on our eyesight. The same with chickenpox. As the dreadful bumps appeared, the itching followed. Our mom made a special salve to smooth on the skin, which also contained yellow sulfur powder. She put socks on our hands to keep the bumps from becoming infected from scratching. It was even worse if the weather was nice and we were confined to the inside of our house. We just wanted it to be over, so we could go outside and play with the other kids.

FOUR

Siblings and Ancestry

BOTH OF MY parents were born in Missouri. They had known one another earlier in life, because both sides of the family lived in Kentucky. My father's ancestry was Scottish and Irish, and my mother's ancestry was Dutch and German. My dad had been a coal miner in the hills of Kentucky and West Virginia. He was ten years older than my mother. My mother's half-sister was married to my dad's late wife's brother. My dad attended school through the second grade, and my mother attended through the fourth grade. They were intelligent and both could read and write. Unfortunately, when they were young, both of them were deprived of a formal education due to hardships within their families. Such was the case with many families of that era. My dad could calculate the answer to a problem faster than someone could do it on paper, but he couldn't show you how he arrived at the answer.

When my parents married, they moved around a lot, and during the Great Depression they were homeless. Of course there were many who were homeless. At that time, they had several children. They did own a car, so as they traveled, my dad worked odd jobs for people. They spent the nights at a safe place. My mom and dad usually slept on the ground, and the children would bed down inside the car. When they moved and settled back in Missouri, my dad continued working as a coal miner. This was a poor man's living, but he was very skilled. When Mick and I were younger, he would sometimes take us with him to the mine during the summer. Our dog, Blackie would go with us, and he would jump off the tipple, and swim in the water at the bottom.

Quite often our dad was hired to create a leather whip which was used in the coal mine to encourage the stubborn mules pull the rail car loaded with coal, up and out of the underground mine. It was a well-known fact that our dad made only the best whips. The mules would travel the rails up and along the tipple. A tipple is a structure going uphill lined with rails on each side. A railroad hopper-car is used at a mine to load the extracted coal for transport up the tipple. From the top of the tipple, the coal was sprayed with water to wash and remove the dust, and then it would be dumped to the ground. Often the mules would stall, and become lazy. The whip was used to urge them on, and stay focused, just as it is with a riding horse.

I often sat at my dad's feet watching as he created this object. The whip was made from strips of leather that attached to a handle. The strips of leather were braided for several feet, and at the very bottom of the whip, our dad placed buckshot which was braided into the strips of leather, creating a sting when striking an object.

My dad served in WWI and as a result, while battling

in France, he was hit by machine gun fire and lost a lung. He received not only the Purple Heart, but also the Silver Star for bravery. The middle of his upper back had a huge crevice in the area where he lost the lung, and whenever he was not wearing a shirt, I would often place my small fist in the crevice. He would tell us war stories, but only later in life did I finally figure out that my dad suffered from what we now term as PTSD. My mother told me while he was in a foxhole with his buddy, rounds from a machine gun entered the fox hole, and his buddy was mortally wounded in the head. He often spent nights replaying this image over and over in his dreams, which no doubt explained his Saturday drinking binges. A lot of people have hang-ups after seeing conflict from war.

All of my grandparents were deceased before I was born. I felt cheated out of this experience. Grandpa Charley was the last one to die. He was my mother's father, and he died about five years before I was born. As I look at his pictures, I can see that Julie, Geri, and I each resembled him. He was not a large man, but he had reddish hair, and deep-set eyes. My mother's mom died shortly after childbirth while still a young woman, only thirty-nine years of age. My dad's mother lived a long life, but his father died when he and his siblings were small. At the time of his death, their mother was also pregnant with her fifth child. She later married Mr. Hensley, and he helped to raise her children. They never had children together.

I will now introduce my siblings from the oldest to the youngest, and provide a little bit of information about each one of them. Otho was my oldest brother, and as I have already established, he was the son of my father and his first wife who died from tuberculosis. He was five years old when my mom and dad married. He had served in the US Army in WWII. He was married to Marie, and they had six children; Susie, Carolyn, Daniel, Peggy, David, and Sheila. Carolyn died as a baby. Although Otho's children were my nieces and nephews, Susie and Danny were very close to my age, and we were more like best friends. I was four months older than Susie. It was exciting when they were around. Susie had beautiful dark hair and her mother used to roll her hair in long curls. I would have died for that hair! I had blonde straight hair, and I would try to wet my hair and twist it to resemble long curls. What a sight that must have been. Otho and Marie are deceased, and Susie passed recently.

Charles is my next oldest brother. He was the one who gave me my name. He was known to the older siblings as the banker of the group, in other words, the money-man. He remains very frugal today at the age of ninety-two. Growing up, he loaned money to his siblings, but they had to pay him back a really good return for his money. He was thrifty and held onto the money he earned. He served in Guam during WWII, and he and his first wife had a son, William, Billy for short, and an infant daughter that died. While Charles was in service, he and his wife divorced, and Billy remained with us for a few years. I am less than two years older than Billy, and at that time I thought we were brother and sister. When Billy was four or five, Charles remarried, and her name was Thelma Jo. They never had children together, but she raised Billy as a loving mother would do. They moved to Minnesota in the 1950s to find work, and remained there until they retired and moved back to Missouri. Thelma Jo passed a few years ago.

Leota was the oldest daughter. In fact, for years I didn't know her name was anything other than "Sister." She had married Squeaky, which was his nickname, when I was two years old. They had a daughter, Betty Ann, who was three years younger than me. They later had a son named John, and a daughter named Phyllis. Betty passed from a crippling disease, leaving an infant daughter. John died from Pancreatic Cancer. Both Squeaky and Leota are deceased.

Squeaky served as the county sheriff for many years. Leota always cooked for the men who were incarcerated, and because she was an excellent cook, we used to joke that everyone tried to be thrown in jail just to eat Leota's cooking.

My brother Al was next. Albert Lester Skinner. Oh, how I adored him. He had a Packard automobile with a rumble seat. He worked for a local soft-drink company that bottled and distributed their drinks. Each day he came home for lunch, and he always brought me small sample bottles of the soda. They were so very tiny, and I used them to play house with my dolls. I was four years old at that time. He spoiled me silly, and after lunch he would pick me up and set me in the rumble seat of his car, and take me for a ride around the block before returning to work. I always said he looked like Gene Autry the singing cowboy, who was best known for his Christmas holiday songs; "Rudolph," "Frosty," "Here Comes Santa Claus," and "Up On The Housetop."

Al married Betty Jane. We called her Jane. She had red hair, and was very small. Al served in the US Army, and they had three children. Teresa was their firstborn, and she had freckles across her nose and a huge smile. Gregg was next, and later they adopted a newborn son, and named him Scott. My heart was broken when my brother lost his life in June, 1984, due to the carelessness of a drunk driver. The previous month, as my birthday gift, my husband took me to Sikeston Missouri to visit Al. I'm thankful that we had that time together. Several years ago Gregg lost his life to cancer.

My next sister was Ilene. We began calling her "Tib" when I was fairly young, and she was always very comical. She could sing country western songs just as well as the artists who recorded them, Patsy Cline in particular. She was always laughing and she could perform a Minnie Pearl skit at the drop of a hat. She married at a young age to Anthony, known to us as Ted. Their first child was a girl, and her name was Brenda. She died very young from Bronchial Pneumonia. They were living in California at that time, but they moved back to Missouri shortly thereafter. Ted had served in the U.S. Navy, and my older sisters envied his black Pea Coat, which was originally designed to be worn by sailors. He was a very handsome young man with red hair, and a bit on the shy side.

They spent most of their married years in Minnesota, having moved there in the 1950s. There was a shortage of jobs in Missouri during those years, so they moved to Minnesota and gained employment. Soon, Charles and his family followed. Deborah was born a few years later, and then Steven, Patricia, and Michelle.

When I was 15 years old, I lived with Tib and Ted. I had gone there for the summer, but I remained the rest of the year before moving back home to Missouri. That was shortly after Patty was born. Patty was nicknamed by her dad. He called her "Peety-Boo-Boo," and I still call her that even today, although she is now sixty years old. When I lived with them, Deb was in the first grade, and Steven was about four years old. Deb lost her battle with cancer several years ago. Both Tib and Ted are deceased as well.

My sister Mary Ella was next after Ilene. She was always the daredevil of the family. She always loved to go exploring around town, and without checking with the owner, would sometimes simply borrow someone else's bicycle if she saw it wasn't being used. She rode off on the bike for long periods of time before returning it. She was always curious about things. Unfortunately, I was not around her as much as my other sisters, because at the age of 13, she went to live with our older sister, and remained there until she graduated from high school. I did, however, spend several summers with Mary and her husband Bob, when I was in high school. She and I presently live within close proximity to one another, and the two of us and our families are extremely close.

Mary and Bob were blessed with six daughters close in age. The daughters are; Marsha, Marla, Dona, Dana, Denise, and Mia. Marsha was always very serious and studious. Marla was always laughing, and her laugh just seemed to come from her toes to her mouth. Marla passed a few years ago. She was the most non-complaining and loving woman I ever knew. She passed not long after her father died, leaving a huge hole in our hearts.

Doris was our next sibling, and she is also deceased. She was married to Gene. As a young woman she was my Sunbeam leader while attending church at The Salvation Army. At that time the church also had a transportation ministry, and this is the method by which we were able to attend. Doris taught me how to sew patches on my Sunbeam vest, and she helped me recite Bible verses. She was my protector at home, helping me with so many things. In our family, the older children helped with the younger ones, so Doris faithfully did this with me. In a number of photos, I am seen standing next to Doris, with her hands on my shoulders. Doris was the mother of several children by two marriages. Roberta, John, Sheila, and Paul are the children of Doris and Gene. The children born to Doris and her second husband John, are Gary, Michael and Michelle (twins), Melissa, Katina, and Jeffrey. Their son Gary passed away, and John is also deceased. Doris remarried to a gentleman named Jack. They had no children together.

Jeweldine, (Julie) and Geraldine, (Geri) are identical twins. When Mick and I were young, we could not pronounce their names. We began calling them Gee-gee and Ginny with a hard "G" sound. I have no idea how the two of us developed these names, but whatever Mick did, I followed along. Through the years while at family gatherings or reunions, the twins would switch clothing in order to fool everyone. Most of the time the trick worked. They were very much alike, and it's quite strange that they both had similar surgeries within the same year. Julie moved to Minnesota to live with our older sister Tib, and while there, she met and married her husband Vernon. Julie and Vernon remained in Minnesota and raised four children; Bruce, Kevin, Mark, and Colleen. While living in Minnesota in 1960, I spent some of my weekends with them. At that time, they had only the oldest two sons. Vernon is deceased and Julie is now married to Harold.

Geri also married at a young age and had a son, Rodney,

and a daughter, Elaine. Later she divorce, and remarried, spending many years as a military wife. She and her husband Ken have a daughter, Robin. Ken is deceased, and Geri is now married to Robert, a man from the south. They live in South Carolina. Geri and I used to lay in bed, and she taught me to spell my name. We worked on this repeatedly. She played "This little piggy" with me, and she would braid my hair. She is also the first one to introduce me to pizza. When she first got married, I spent a few days with her, and she and her husband had a spider monkey. His name was Timmy, and he liked to swing from the furniture by his tail, and to also chase their cat. Monkeys have always fascinated me, especially their hands and fingers.

The next younger sister was Dorothy. We called her Dot. She was married briefly and later divorced. After a number of years of being single, she married Bill, and together they had four children; Theresa, William, Darenda, and Catrena. They lived in Pennsylvania for many years before relocating to Missouri. Bill passed a number of years ago, and Dottie died ten years ago.

Carl is our youngest brother. Jokingly, I always said that he was born just to tease all of his sisters. He is 18 months my senior. His nickname is "Mickey," and none of us have ever called him Carl. Most of us called him "Mick." When he began school, he informed the teacher if she called him Carl, he would not come to school. He was the most likely to tattle on the girls to our dad. Because he was the only boy within the younger group of children, he had his own bed, which I felt was not fair.

Mick was the last one to leave home. He married Joanita at the age of 29, and they had two children. Michael was the first-born and Amy was the second child. They moved to Tennessee when the children were young, and later to Texas. Mick was always a truck driver. He is 77 years old, and is still driving truck for a living. He and I remain extremely close, stuck like glue. Once while we were small, I lost my toothbrush. He told me I could borrow his. That's a true brother!

Uncle Gilbert and Aunt Lillie lived in Quincy, Illinois, and Lillie was our mother's sister. Several times a year they made the trip from Quincy to Moberly for a visit. They had a son, Raymond, who never married. We thought that they were rich because they owned a laundry and dry cleaning business. Gilbert and Lillie never drove, so when they came to visit, Raymond always did the driving. Gilbert and Raymond always wore the snap down Newsboy caps, and they drove a forty-something Plymouth that was immaculate. I thought it odd that the rear doors opened backward, like I had seen in the Al Capone movies.

Whenever our aunt and uncle came to visit, Aunt Lillie usually asked Raymond to drive her to the grocery to buy a few things for dinner. She always took me along with them. She purchased the same things every time, which were salad ingredients and French dressing. She always bought a square, two-layer Dolly Madison white layer cake with fluffy icing sprinkled with coconut. I looked forward to this. We couldn't afford some of these items, and I was especially fond of the French salad dressing as well as the cake. This particular coconut cake is still an all-time favorite of mine.

Aunt Lillie was a few years older than our mom. She had the habit of slipping money into my mother's apron pocket for her to spend on something extra that she might not be able to afford. They were very generous. Aunt Lillie wore makeup and jewelry, and my mother did not. She wore an Eastern Star pin, necklace, and earrings. She gave me butterscotch hard candy and root beer logs. She and my mother corresponded by mail, and I always wrote her a note and slipped in into the envelope with my mother's letter. She sometimes sent me a crisp one-dollar bill when she wrote back to me.

Our cousin Raymond had a great many toys from his childhood, which were in pristine condition. Because he was now older, he began bringing some of these items to us. I remember the Little Big Books, and in the top corners were pictures. I liked the Red Ryder ones. If you thumbed through the pages fast enough, it looked as though the pictures were moving in frames. He gave us his train, complete with the buildings, signs, and trees posted along the interlocking train tracks. Another one of the items was an RCA wind-up Victrola, and lots of seventy-eight speed records. We had to wind up the Victrola with a crank handle. It had a speaker where the sound came out, and on the speaker was engraved a picture of a sitting dog. I recall that one of the records was "Turkey in the Straw."

Raymond was also quite skilled at roller skating. On occasion when they came for a visit, Raymond seized the opportunity to take my older siblings to the roller rink, but I never went with them. I could not skate and I was afraid I would fall and hurt myself. I would just as soon hang out with my aunt and uncle. Raymond also gave Mick his treasured bicycle. Mick was so proud of that bike. I begged him to take me for rides, and our parents forced him to do so, but when we got out of the sight of our parents, he began doing bicycle tricks to scare me and I ended up getting off the bike and walking back home. Who in their right mind wants their younger sister riding on their bike for everyone to see anyway? When we argued, I tried to kick him. He would hold the top of my head, and pushing me out, he distanced himself from me so that I couldn't reach him, and I would be flailing in mid-air. He began laughing at me, which made me even angrier.

As I have already pointed out, our dad was very strict and did not allow dancing. One day, my sisters, Julie, Geri, and Dot, decided to crank up the Victrola that Raymond had given us, set it on the front porch, and dance in the side yard. Mick warned them that they were going to get in trouble. I don't know if they purposely did it because there was a crew of young men who were working on the road and they wanted to flirt or not, but they were out of the sight of our mother, so she was unaware of what they were doing. Unfortunately, my dad came home just in time to see what they were doing and they were reprimanded.

Our dogs were such a huge part of the family, and so were our cats. We ran and played with the dogs, in attempt to teach them tricks. The first dog I remember was Penny, and I remember that he could sit up on his haunches until he had permission to get down. My brother and sisters would put our dad's glasses on Penny's face, and he remained still until someone gave him permission to take a break. He hid under the porch when he heard the dog catcher coming. The dog catcher drove a wagon pulled by a horse. He had a large cage on the wagon, in which he would place the dogs. Penny was also the dog that liked to chase the hand-cars on the railroad tracks.

I was not yet in school, but Penny loved to go to school with the older kids. We did not live far from school. The kids would coax him to climb the steps to the slide, and then they put him on the slick metal and let him slide down, all the while trying to hang on with his toenails. When he was close to the bottom, he jumped off and ran back to the bottom of the steps, ready to climb the ladder again. All of the kids loved our dog. He would perk up his ears when he heard the kids on the playground, and he returned to school for both recesses. After the afternoon recess, he remained close to the playground waiting for school to be dismissed, ready to follow my siblings back home. Penny died of old age months before our house burned.

Our older neighbors had a black Cocker Spaniel whose name was Corky, but Corky had died. One day as Mick and I were looking out the window, and into the yard of that same neighbor's yard, when we noticed another black Cocker Spaniel. I said to Mick, "Oh, look, Corky is back."

To that, Mick replied, "That is not Corky. That is Corky's brother-in-law."

Blackie was our next dog. Mick claimed that Blackie belonged to him, but while living in Huntsville Missouri, he was given to our family by our neighbor Earl Wolverton. Mick enjoyed playing cowboys and Indians, and he pretended that Blackie was "Rin Tin Tin," the dog from the movies. Blackie was a great at protecting the family, and he was afraid of nothing, challenging any dog who looked antagonistic. Eventually he went blind and became very aggressive. Our dad was afraid he would hurt someone, so he had to put him down. We never had another dog after Blackie.

My sister Dot had a female cat that she named Mamie. The cat was named after President Eisenhower's wife. Mamie liked to sleep with us, but knowing she was due to have babies, our mother fixed a nesting-box for her on the back porch. One morning we awoke to tiny crying sounds, only to discover that Mamie had given birth to her litter right there in our bed. Our mother was very upset. Dot had sneaked her into the bedroom, and into our bed. She made Dot wash the bedding, and also made her put the litter of newborn kittens in the nesting box on the back porch. Dot always had a great love for feline fur babies, and she was forever bringing home a stray.

As the youngest, I will admit that I was a bit spoiled. I don't mean spoiled with material things, but rather by receiving attention. Being the closest in age with Mick, we have that special brother and sister relationship. Now that we have both joined the over-the-hill gang, we look back and laugh at some of the things that we did, or at least participated in doing. I never received a spanking, and I don't believe I ever deserved one, but that's strictly my opinion. Whenever I saw trouble brewing, I found a hole to crawl into, so to speak. Our dad was strict with discipline, and in order to punish the guilty wrongdoer, he punished every single kid he thought might be responsible. When our dad was gone, and someone misbehaved, our mother would say, "You just wait until your Daddy gets home." Of course I don't think she told on them every time. Although our dad used stronger discipline than our mom, I think once my dad stopped drinking, the method by which he disciplined, lessened as well.

FIVE

Binges and Deliverance

I WATCHED MY dad's behavior throughout my childhood, and on many a Saturday morning he left the house, and returned late afternoon or early evening. Sometimes he would walk the tracks and cross over them as he got close to town. If he walked home, he also returned by way of the tracks. Many times we could see him returning home, because he would stagger down the railroad tracks, often falling down. My mother then would yell at some of the older kids to go help her bring him the rest of the way home. They picked him up, and supported his arms while guiding him the rest of the way home, and he would be staggering to stay upright.

I didn't know much about it, but I know that it made me very sad. I didn't like the way my daddy smelled or slurred his words. I loved both my parents dearly, and I never took sides, but I know it embarrassed my mother and my older siblings. I know she was worried from the time he left, until the time he arrived back home. I watched the despair on my mother's face. He had spent the day drinking and shooting craps with his drinking buddies along one section of downtown known as the "Levee." It was not a good place for women and children to go, but drinking men would gather there. Since he gambled, my mother never knew if he had won or lost money, and if he had lost, what would she feed the family the next week? He was a very proud man, never accepting help from anyone, but he definitely had a problem. My mother was surely a saint by enduring this behavior, and she did everything she could to care for us. Once in a while our dad took our mom to a movie on a Friday night. They rode the bus, and when they came home, she usually brought us a box of popcorn to split the next morning. The older kids were left in charge of the younger ones.

On one occasion when our parents were at the movies, the older girls decided they were going to make homemade fudge. Our mother was quite frugal when it came to using her ingredients for cooking, and there would certainly be no wasting because we couldn't afford it. I don't think they followed her recipe exactly so, because it never did get firm. The girls made us eat all of the "spoon fudge" before our parents got home. I think everyone had a stomach ache afterward, and I don't think we wanted the popcorn as we normally would have.

Even though we didn't have a large variety of foods in our diets, our mother could make anything taste good. I always told everyone that my family was the inventor of soul food. We ate from our garden, and we ate wild game, including raccoon, as well as turtle, rabbit, and squirrel. My mother could take the shell off a turtle faster than anyone we knew. Someone would kill the turtle while she boiled water over an outside fire. When the water boiled, she would hold the turtle under the water, and the shell just seemed to turn loose. She then cut up the meat, and fried it, which was very tasty. We ate beef tongue, pork brains, pig ears and pigtails. This may sound unpleasant, but when you have very little, these foods were welcomed. My dad used to say, "What won't kill you will surely fatten you." I always said we ate anything that didn't eat us first.

On Sunday we often had chicken and dumplings, which made an adequate amount of food. If that were the case, our dad would stop at the poultry house on Saturday as he returned home, whether he had been drinking and gambling or not. He bought a live fat hen, and they would tie its legs together. He rode the city bus home as he held the hen on the floor. Sometimes he was a bit more inebriated than other times. I was told the story that once while he was riding the bus, the hen got away from him and was flying around, and it scared all of the ladies on the bus. I'm sure the bus driver was certainly glad to see him exit the bus at his stop.

My mother was a Bible-believing Christian woman. She also had a beautiful voice. She taught me to carry harmony by the time I was seven. This would play a large part in the rest of my life. She passed her musical talent to her children, because to my knowledge, we were all gifted with an ability to sing. As a group, the youngest five would sing songs a cappella. We liked to attend church where we were asked to sing, and three of my sisters also composed a song that we would sometimes sing at church. Our mother sang ballads, and later in life I discovered that these songs were typical bluegrass music. She knew these songs, having lived many of her childhood years in the hills of Kentucky, where bluegrass music originated.

Mommy, as I called her, would tell us Bible stories, and she would talk to us about God. She was of the Presbyterian faith, but she did not attend church. Although I honored my mother and father, we never prayed. I can't speak for her private life, but I would like to believe that she did pray. She had very few clothes and felt that she had nothing worthy of wearing to church, so she just didn't go. She did, however, encourage her children to attend. The choice of where to attend was strictly up to us.

At this point in my life, many of the older children had either left home, or had gone to live with other siblings. I began attending Immanuel Baptist Church. I continued finding this man Jesus to be quite fascinating. I became friends with the pastor's daughter. The pastor was Russell Doyle. There were several ladies who usually invited me to sit with them during church. One of the ladies was widowed and lived just across the back alley, and a few houses down from where we lived. This lady's name was Ms. Broaduss, and she had made me a gored skirt of different colors of her leftover fabric, but it was very pretty. As I sat beside these "blue-haired" ladies, I admired their clothing and jewelry, and as I smelled their cologne, I wished that my mother could have these things. Ms. Broaduss opened her Bible, found the text, smiled at me, and placed it on my lap. I never had a Bible of my own, but she allowed me to follow the words with my finger as the preacher read them to the congregation.

My father never attended church, but he was very strict. I think this must have come from his upbringing.

His mother was a very godly woman, staunch and firm. She must have taught the Bible to her children, because he could quote some of the scripture, but mostly out of context. We weren't allowed to wear shorts, makeup, dance, or play cards. At that time I found great irony in his beliefs because of his own drinking and gambling, but I didn't sass back.

I recall a certain day quite some time after my dad had stopped drinking. He went to town on Saturday, and it was later in the afternoon when came home. He was actually playing a trick on our mom. He always wore bibbed overalls, and he carried his wallet snapped down in the bib. He had removed his money from his wallet, hidden it in his boot, and placed his wallet back in the bib of his overalls.

When our mother saw him staggering, she assumed he was drunk. He pretended to fall before reaching our house. Upon seeing this, she yelled for the older kids to come and help her. She said, "It's your dad, and he's been drinking again."

My siblings went the short distance with our mother to bring our dad home. Everyone was given instructions to lift underneath his arms, head, and legs and help carry him the rest of the way. Before that, she checked his wallet. Very upset, she commented, "Well, he has lost all of his money again."

Everyone held onto his arms and legs as they began carrying him, but they had not gotten very far when he began laughing out loud. At that point, our mother gave a command. She said, "Okay kids, drop him!" I think it was a very long time before she would speak to him, and I don't think he ever tried that trick again.

At the age of 13, I became involved in the younger youth

group at church. I also attended most other functions, such as Sunday morning Worship Service, Wednesday night prayer meetings, and anything else that was planned throughout the week. My close group of friends were likewise involved. I attended Bible School during the summer, and helped with the young children. Pastor Doyle resigned, and when he left, our new pastor became Jimmy Maidment. I loved my new pastor and his wife, and when his wife had something important to do, I volunteered to go to their home to watch their three year-old son, Steven.

While in the Maidment home I saw so much about the love of Jesus, that I began to have questions about what it meant to be a Christian. I thought if you believed in Jesus, then that automatically made you a Christian. Of course I loved Jesus and believed in God, and most certainly I wanted to go to Heaven when I died, but I began to question if there was something else I needed to do. I began asking questions, and having discussions with the pastor's wife. I really liked being there. She was kind and loving, and she worded things so that I could easily understand. Sometimes they invited me to stay for a meal, and we would always pray before we ate, which was something we didn't do at home. It made me long to know more about Him.

The month before my 14th birthday there was a revival taking place at our church, and the youth was asked to go door-to-door handing out information pamphlets. I felt happy I had been asked to help out. During those years, revivals were held seven days a week for two full weeks. Each afternoon, I rushed home from school to do my homework so that I wouldn't miss a single night of the revival. I sincerely believe that God had ordained this exact time in my life. On one of the nights during the first week, the Holy Spirit convicted me and I asked Jesus to come into my heart and be my Savior. It was pretty emotional. That was on April 14, 1959, and two weeks later, I was baptized by immersion. My mother came to watch my baptism, and I was so happy that she did. My life would never be the same. I remember that we walked to church, because my mother didn't drive. Although it seemed quite a distance, it was about a 15 minute walk, which was less than a mile.

Being sure that my mother was a Christian, I was equally convinced that my dad did not have a relationship with Jesus. I began telling him that he needed to invite Jesus into his heart. He had stopped drinking, so he was no longer consumed by his Saturday trips to the downtown Levee. I never knew what brought about this change, but I think it must have been by a very strong insistence by my mother. He told me when he thought he could be good enough, he would do that. I then went on to explain to him that no one could ever be good enough, and that salvation was only given to us as a free gift from God. If you don't accept that gift, then you aren't saved, and if you aren't saved, then you can't go to Heaven. I shared with him the simple message of God from the viewpoint of a young fourteen year-old girl. A seed must have been planted, because the year before he died of Black Lung, he accepted Jesus Christ as his Savior.

Black Lung was caused from working in the coal mines. There were so many wasted years. My dad was a good man, and he would do anything for anyone, and I knew he believed in God, but he had not settled the account of his life with God until this point. This happened the year before he died in February, 1974, at the age of 75. My mother was ten years younger than my dad, and she died in June, 1977, at the age of 68. I was 28 when my dad died, and I was 32 when my mom passed. Many years remained when I needed them, but I always felt in my heart, that they were with me.

My sister Mary and I were the only ones in our family to graduate from high school. Most of my siblings either dropped out of school to go to work, or to marry early. I don't mean this to be critical, but to prove that education doesn't just come by way of books, but it also comes from experience. I have had, and still have, very intelligent sisters and brothers. I don't feel that a person ever stops learning. Our parents did not have formal educations, yet still they were both very wise, and skilled.

I always had a hunger and thirst for learning. I never had to worry about good grades, because learning seemed to come easy for me. I was always on the Honor Roll, and later, the Scholarship Society. I was blessed with wonderful teachers, and I have retained so much of what I learned throughout school. When we were children and brought our report cards home from school, our parents always asked if we had done our very best. If we answered positively, then there was no problem. Only we could be the judge of that.

Each school year, we were obligated to take the Iowa Achievement Test. This test was simply an evaluation of a child's knowledge of what they had learned in school, and it was not a cognitive or IQ test. Despite the name, at that time many state and private schools administered Iowa Tests. Our Missouri Education system has since switched to MAP testing. This is simply the acronym for Measure of Academic Progress. During my sixth grade, the teacher announced to the class that one of her students had tested very high on the Iowa Achievement Test in the area of mathematics. That sixth-grade student had scored tenth grade, second month. She then went on to announce my name. I almost fainted, and because I was shy, I could feel my face grow red and my legs go weak. "Oh, brother," I wanted to crawl under the desk. Because of this, nobody would want to be my friend, especially the boys. They already called me "Book Worm," and I was never picked when we played a game, and now I was humiliated. Fortunately the kids either forgot, or didn't make it an issue, because I didn't lose any of my close friends over the announcement. It was no doubt a bigger issue to me than it was to them. Neither did it make a difference when choosing sides for the games, because I was still not picked, and I was always last, so I didn't lose a thing by being humiliated.

I can recall some of the kids at school who played baseball very well. Several of the girls could play equally as well as the boys. When choosing sides, they were usually chosen first. I especially remember Roberta Stroud, Betty Spicer, and Helen Hayes. Not only was Betty Spicer great at baseball during elementary school, she was also good at sports in high school.

The Langdon family lived about five houses down, and they had three sons. Both their mom and dad worked outside the home. Dickie was in my class, and he didn't like school. He struggled with learning, and also with his homework. His parents would not allow him to go outside and play with the other kids until he completed his homework. Since both parents worked, their sons were given a generous allowances to help around their house.

On many occasions, Dickie would suggest that if I

agreed to help him with his homework, he would buy me candy. Well, I was all about that sort of deal, so we would meet on the sidewalk steps, or front porch, and he would have a bag of Red Hots or a bag of Tootsie Rolls to pay me back for helping him. As this progressed, he grew more and more dependent on me, and I became more dependent on the candy. My parents found out about the scheme, and ended our arrangement by telling me that I was supposed to help others without expecting anything back. This was a great lesson for my life, and I learned it well, even though at that time I didn't like it.

The Langdon boys invited Mick and me to watch television, and we also watched television with the Fox children, who were also our neighbors and had three kids close to our age. We waited until three o'clock in the afternoon to meet and watch Howdy Doody at either of their homes. Both of these families had agreed that Mick and I could come and watch television before supper. The networks were not on the air until three o'clock each afternoon. Instead, there was a test pattern of circles with a snowy screen. As soon as the network would come on the air, and the show began, we would hear them say, "Hey kids, what time is it?" The theme song would begin, "It's Howdy Doody time."

At midnight, the networks always displayed an American flag waving in the breeze, and played "The Star Spangled Banner" before retiring from the air. We knew the day had ended for broadcast, and would not resume until the next day. When the next day arrived, we perched ourselves before the screen to welcome the broadcast at precisely three o'clock in the afternoon.

On most Friday nights, we went to our oldest brother's house to watch the Friday Night Cavalcade of Sports, which was boxing. My dad loved to watch boxing, and it was televised each week. We began to familiarize ourselves with each one of the boxers, and each of us had our favorites. We watched and cheered and told the boxer where to punch, and the list goes on. My dad sat in a chair, and rocked back and forth as if he was in the ring trying to avoid the punches. When the boxing was over, it was time to drive home with at least one sleepy kid.

My brother, Charles, and my sister, Tib, who were both living in Minnesota at the time, devised a plan. They informed us that their families were planning a trip back to Missouri with a surprise for our parents. When they arrived, they unloaded something from their vehicle. The surprise was a television, and as with the early televisions, the screen was nearly round. Even though the picture was considered to be black and white, the screen itself was actually greenish in color. They had also purchased an antenna which was to be installed on the outside of the house. It was in sections and had to be fitted together with wires running through the bottom portion of the window, and connected to the television inside. I was so excited, I could hardly wait. I can also remember that each day after receiving the television, my mother watched "I Love Lucy," and she laughed more than I had ever seen her laugh.

I think my mom was almost as pleased with the television, as she was the day when my dad went to town and returned home with a new gas stove for the kitchen, which was yet another thing that made me happy. Life was certainly improving, and we were moving up in the world.

Of course my dad declared that biscuits weren't quite the same as they had been on the coal stove, but he ate them anyway. Watching television had also become a favorite pastime. Who knew that in a few short years, my mom and dad would become addicted to "The Edge of Night," as he rushed home each afternoon, so that they could watch it together? We all laughed about this, because they carried on conversations about the show as if it were real.

SIX

Hometown Perks

THERE WAS A movie theater located in downtown Moberly. It was the Grand Theater, and it certainly was grand to me. When we were kids, the only time we were ever able to go to a movie was on Saturday morning. We could gain free admission if we had five 7-Up bottle caps or five Stamper milk carton tops. There was a 7-Up distributor in our town, and also a Stamper Dairy, and I'm sure they helped fund the showing of the movies. For lunch each day, we were served the small half-pint cartons of milk, and even if we packed our lunch, we could purchase a carton of milk for a penny. We flattened the carton and took it home each day to rinse it out and save it for free admission to the movie on Saturday morning. If we wanted popcorn or soda, we had to pick up pop bottles and sell them at the grocery store.

We never received an allowance, so as we pulled the small wagon we searched the ditches throughout our town for bottles that had been discarded. We washed them, and took them to the store where we would receive two cents for each bottle. The distributor would then reimburse the owner of the grocery store. This was also what I did when I wanted to buy penny candy. I think BB Bats were my favorite, but I also loved Banana Bikes and Tootsie Rolls. I stood gazing at the candy through the glass on the front of the counter, trying to make up my mind. Jawbreakers were nice too, because they lasted much longer than most other kinds of candy.

Reed Street was the main street running through downtown. T.W. Kamp Jewelry was located at the far southwest end of the street. To coincide with each season or holiday, they changed the decorations in the storefront window, but the scenes were always animated. I was captivated by the movement and motion of the animations, so I stood and stared. The scene was so magical, especially at Christmas.

Patterson's Department Store sold only the most up-to-date clothing. As I recall, I purchased only a few of their items. I noticed the teenagers going in and out of Mear's Drug Store as they gathered in groups like best friends do, and they sipped on a Coca Cola and played popular music on a juke box. The drug store sold two sizes of Coca Cola. The small one was a nickel, and the large one was a dime. I promised myself that in a few years I would also to do this with my friends.

My older sisters were always wanting to earn money or win prizes. They most likely used the money to buy makeup without our dad knowing. About once a year they would go door to door selling Motto Cards to earn money or win prizes. These cards were fairly large, and could be hung on the wall. They were covered with a layer of glitter. There was a Bible verse inscribed on each one, and the card glowed in the dark. There were purple ones, and royal blue one. At the time I read the verses, I wondered where these verses were in the Bible, and exactly what each verse meant. Because my sisters were so eager to earn money, they went door-to-door attempting to sell just about anything. They sold Red Clover Salve, and Dr. Sayman's Salve, an antibiotic ointment and they also sold punch cards.

When we moved to Collins Avenue, there was an older man and woman who lived on Hinton Avenue, behind where we lived. Their name was Mr. and Mrs. Courier, and a few years later, Mrs. Courier became the victim of a stroke and was confined to her bed. When we first became their neighbors, she seemed just fine. She asked me if she could hire me to occasionally come and wash her dishes. I agreed, and it was always on a Saturday morning. I really believe the actual reason she wanted me to come, was because she missed her two grandchildren who rarely visited her, although they lived in the same town. She seemed starved for conversation, and I'm sure she missed them.

Mrs. Courier had a number of glass medicine bottles which she kept in the kitchen on the lower shelf of a pie safe. Because the bottles became very sticky from the syrupy part of the medicine, she instructed me how to carefully remove the lids of each bottle one by one, wiping the bottles and lids with a clean damp cloth. To me, it seemed that she took an awfully lot of medicine. She was pleased with my work, so she often called on me to help her. She paid me 35 cents each time I went.

After the stroke, things seemed like they were in a state of limbo. I felt it was time that I went to visit Mrs. Courier on my own. My mother had gone to visit her a number of times because Mr. Courier had hired my mother to do some of his mending. Mostly she mended his bibbed overalls, but my mother also helped with a few other things, such as changing Mrs. Courier's bedding. My mother did a wonderful job of patching, so this became routine.

On one particular day, Mr. Courier was getting out of his old pickup, so I walked across the alley to talk to him. He asked if I would like to see his wife. I nodded, and he invited me in, leading me to the living room where she lay in a twin bed. This was the first time I had seen her after the stroke. It was kind of dark in the room with her curtains drawn shut, and it was difficult to understand Mrs. Courier, but it didn't take me long to combat that problem. Her mouth seemed twisted, and as she reached out her hand toward me, she motioned for me to sit down in the chair next to her bed. Her fingers seemed more twisted than I had remembered. It was quite evident that she was horribly afflicted with arthritis. Why had I not noticed this before?

Mrs. Courier grew more comfortable with my being there, and sometimes I slipped across the alleyway just to sit at her bedside and talk to her and read articles to her from the magazines they received in the mail. As is often a result of a stroke, she laughed out loud for no apparent reason. I didn't know why she did this, so I asked my mom, and she explained that emotions are also affected when someone has had a stroke. Mrs. Courier asked if I would cut her toenails. I really didn't know what to say, but I remembered the story in the Bible about Jesus washing some men's feet. I figured if Jesus could touch someone else's feet, then so could I, so I told her I would, and this became a monthly duty as well.

I took a wash pan and fill it with soapy water, bathed her

feet, and trimmed her toenails with small clippers. I tried to be very careful. Her toes were also twisted, and her nails were hard and brittle. I filed them so that they were smooth, so as to keep the edges from being jagged. I was proud when the task was accomplished. This was important to her, for when her toenails were long, they would get caught on her blankets and become bothersome. Although I didn't expect pay for this gesture, she insisted that I take the money. Her husband placed another 35 cents into my palm. He told me he was grateful, and that he was afraid he would cut her toes because his hands were so shaky.

When I told my parents what I had done, my brother Mick overheard me, and began laughing. He was making fun of me for cutting Mrs. Courier's toenails, as if that was something degrading. It wasn't long before he told all the neighborhood kids what I had done, and they also laughed at me which made me cry. I was teased by the others but I soon began defending what I had done, telling them that it was something God probably expected me to do, and that He would be happy I was doing this. Soon they stopped pestering me about it.

My mother also did ironing for other families. I recall that she charged ten cents for each item. I sprinkled each piece for her with a soda bottle filled with water. The bottle had a silver rounded aluminum cap, with small holes to sprinkle the water. The cap was stuck down into the neck of the bottle by a cork which fit snugly and made it secure. After I sprinkled the clothes, I rolled them tightly to keep them damp. I layered them in a wooden clothes basket and tucked a towel over them to keep them damp, ready to be ironed.

At school we had been learning about the U.S. Government. The 1956 Presidential Election was close at hand, and in my class at school we took a poll, voting between Republican President Dwight D. Eisenhower, who was running for reelection against Democrat Adlai Stevenson, the former Illinois governor, whom he had defeated four years earlier. My dad was a very strong Republican, so he was voting for Eisenhower. I remember that my dad allowed me to stay up very late as we listened for the election results to come in on our radio, because I told him our class had voted. Of course my dad was very happy to learn that President Eisenhower would serve a second term.

Shortly afterward, we received word that our neighbor, Mr. Hess, had suddenly passed away. This was a very sad time for all of our neighbors along Collins Avenue. Mr. and Mrs. Hess were great people and great neighbors, having lived in the same house many years. My dad had become close friends with Mr. Hess after moving back to Moberly. They spent a lot of time together even though Mr. Hess was older. My dad also knew a number of members of Mr. Hess' family.

The funeral home made plans to bring Mr. Hess' body to his home to await his funeral. Another person was to sit with the body, even through the night, while the family rested. Friends and family also dropped in throughout the day. My dad was one of those who volunteered to sit with the body, as this was an old custom. The act of sitting with the body was called a "wake," and was done out of respect for the deceased. That failed to make much sense to me. At eleven, I didn't know very much about death, because I was too young to have known anyone who had died except my youngest brother and my baby niece. I didn't know if it meant they were guarding the body, or just what it meant. I remembered the story when Jesus died and they posted guards at the entrance of the tomb. After the funeral was over, my parents tried to be available to help Mrs. Hess in any way they could.

At Halloween, Mrs. Hess had a special Halloween treat for Mick and me. She gave us each a really large candy bar. Our parents allowed Mick and me to go trick-or-treating, and they knew that Mick would protect me. We each took a small pillowcase, because we knew we would come home with a lot of candy and we didn't want to risk a broken bag from the weight of so many apples that many people always passed out to the kids. Sometimes other neighbor kids went with us. We went all over town knocking on doors. I watched to see if the residents were handing out apples, and instead of holding out my bag, I would reach out and take it myself and lay it in the bottom of the pillowcase. I disliked apples being dropped into my bag and breaking or crushing my candy. It was usually late when we returned home, but in those days kids were pretty safe, especially when they were with a group. I could now have my sugar-fix for many days to come. Normally we did receive a lot of apples, so we took them home to our mother, and she used them to bake a pie or two.

Our family seemed content to live on Collins Avenue for the past three or so years, so my parents bought a small house on the opposite side of the street, and just a little bit west. We moved next door to Mrs. Hess, the recent widow. Our days of moving were finally over, at least while I was still at home. My parents knew their neighbors, and there were always plenty of men with whom my dad could visit and talk.

That summer, Mrs. Hess' granddaughter came to visit for part of the summer. Her name was Brenda, and she was my age. We had fun together, and we also ate a lot of fresh cucumbers from the garden. I had never seen anyone eat so many raw cucumbers, but she ate the peeling as well, which I did not like to do.

Soon it would be the start of the school year, and I would be entering grade six. I was beginning to develop and mature, so I paid more attention to things my mother was teaching me, and less on childish things. She told me I was becoming a woman, but I wasn't really sure I wanted to do that. I didn't think I was ready just yet for that. Did that mean that I couldn't go outside and play with other kids? It would have been so much easier if I still had a sister at home to explain things to me. I was always close to my sisters, even though I loved my mother.

That was the same year when my young nephew lived with us for a while. He was soon to be a toddler and he was adorable. Each day I rushed home from school, to take Rodney from his crib and to start playing with him. He was teething, so I gave him ginger snap cookies. I took him outside and tied a towel around his waist. I gave him a cardboard box to push, and he held onto the box pushing it up and down the sidewalk. This is how he learned to walk. Some of the neighbors came outside to watch his daily progress, and they cheered for him.

Once in a while my sister, Dot, came home for the weekend. She had been married briefly at the age of 16, but she had gotten a divorce. She was much too young for marriage, and was subjected to abuse. At this time, she lived in Kirksville, Missouri, which was a little over an hour north of Moberly. Kirksville was home to a state teacher's college. She lived on her own, and worked in a sanitarium, which was a facility for the treatment of people who have a chronic illness. She didn't have a car, so she rode the Greyhound Bus home, and our dad went to the bus station to pick her up. Since she was working and earning money, she bought some really pretty clothes. Of course none of them fit me. Dot was a pretty young woman, and her looks attracted many young men who wanted to date her; however she was careful who she dated.

During the weekends she was home, Dot talked to me and gave me advice. She was very tactful, but sometimes the conversations made me blush. She gave me pointers on my hair, my clothes, fashion, and my posture. I talked to her about what was important to me, and she hugged me and told me how proud she was of me, and that someday I would be a great wife and mother.

When I reached seventh grade, our Health and Science class taught us about the human anatomy, and other strictly private matters. The boys and the girls took separate classes, so I sort of understood what my sister was trying to tell me. I was so glad to be in a class with other girls while we were being taught, rather than being face-to-face with my sister.

I was never invited for sleepovers until I reached high school. Neither did I invite other girls to spend the night at my house. I was not popular, and I did not run around with any of the popular girls. I did not dress like them and I did not talk like them. Most of my friends were those from church. I think they felt the same way that I did, so we just hung out together at church, especially after choir practice on Wednesday night. During those days, teachers never gave homework on Wednesday night because in our town, there were a great number of kids who attended Wednesday night church services. During the summer, the youth from various churches gathered for a service at Rothwell Park. We roasted hotdogs, had a devotional, and sang familiar "camp songs" together while toasting marshmallows.

SEVEN

Lost In the Pages

I ALWAYS LOVED reading, and my parents allowed me to walk downtown to the Carnegie Public Library by myself, which was in downtown Moberly. Normally, I brought home an armload of books, and within a few days I had read all of them, so I asked to go back for more. My dad swore I was going to ruin my eyesight, and although I didn't argue back, I knew that wasn't going to happen. I found that I could get lost within the pages of the books, and I could travel anywhere and see anything through the eyes of someone else. When I was younger, my mother had suggested I read a book which was *The Boxcar Children*. She told me she had also read it as a child. Without saying so, I was surprised that a book could be around that long, but I truly did love it. I believe it is in existence still yet today.

Some of my favorite books were the *Nancy Drew Mysteries*, *The Hardy Boys*, and any of the *Candy Striper* books. I was fascinated with *The Diary of Anne Frank*. I suppose that was because I attended school with a sister and brother who were of the Jewish faith. One day our teacher asked the sister to share with our class, some of the things about temple worship. There was not a temple in Moberly, so in order to attend, the family traveled to Columbia, Missouri, which was 35 miles south. She told us about Hanukkah, and why she did not celebrate the Gentile Christmas, or participate in the Christmas program at school. I was a bit confused, but I didn't ask questions. I later read about this, and also about the Maccabees and their revolt against an evil man who was persecuting the Jewish people in Jerusalem, and how God provided enough oil to burn the Menorah continuously in the Temple for eight days without running out.

I also discovered a book entitled *The Greatest Story Ever Told*. Once I began reading the story, it seemed to come alive. It is the story of Jesus, from his birth in Bethlehem to His death and resurrection. The book brings out different aspects of Jesus life, including the execution of all the newborn males in Egypt, Jesus' baptism by John the Baptist, and the betrayal by Judas after the Last Supper, which eventually led to Jesus' crucifixion and miraculous resurrection and ascension into heaven. I was mesmerized, and although I had read of this in the Bible, it becomes much different and more real when reading it in story form. Somehow in my mind, God was always with us, however He was somewhere out there in space, and far away, and we really couldn't connect to Him. This book made Him so real, and made my understanding much fuller.

The *Little House* books by Laura Ingalls Wilder were favorites as well. The books were geared toward a younger age, but even at my age, the books were fascinating. Who would have ever thought these books would exist over the years, and be made into a television series? The same books I had read as a child were also available for my children to read.

Toward the middle of summer, my mother began having some female issues and the doctor insisted she stay in bed for a number weeks. I did not really know what was happening, but I knew every few days the doctor would come and give her a shot. My dad said something about my mom's hemoglobin, and I would now have to help him in the kitchen. At this point in my life I did not know a thing about cooking. I loved to wash dishes, but that is as far as it went.

The next morning, my dad went about showing me how to make biscuits, with my mother instructing us from her bed. I was very willing, but I know that we could have used those biscuits to play baseball because they were extremely hard. Within the first week I learned to make biscuits that could pass his test. Next, he was going to show me how to fry bacon. I asked him how much grease I should put in the skillet. By now, you have a general idea of how our cooking lessons went.

I learned to change the sheets on my parent's bed by having my mother roll to one side, remove the sheet from that side, and she would roll back to the other side so I could finish the task. I was able to put clean sheets on the bed in the same manner, without her having to get up from bed. My mom told me she was proud of me, and sometimes in the afternoon, I would lay down on the bed next to her and read as the breeze flowed through the room from the open windows. It felt good to snuggle, and to fluff up her pillows to make her comfortable. We laid there and talked, and I asked her questions about her childhood. In a few weeks, she was up and feeling better, and her problem seemed to be resolved.

At church, we usually held a back-to-school party to celebrate the end of summer. We could invite anyone we wanted, even if they didn't attend Immanuel Baptist Church. I always had a long list of those whom I could invite, and we always had a fun time. This was such a good time to reach out to those who didn't attend church, hoping that they would begin. I was asked to bake a cake for the party that year. I remember asking my dad if he would please go to the store and buy a Betty Crocker Marble Cake Mix. My mother never used cake mixes, but since this was my first, I needed for it to be perfect. My mom showed me how to grease and flour the two round pans, and how to gauge the amount of batter in each pan to make them both the same size. She taught me to wash the eggs before I cracked the shell, just in case some of the shell fell into the eggs. She showed me how to crack the shell gently, one by one, without poking my finger through the shell.

When the layers were finished baking and cooled, she taught me how to make her delicious buttercream icing. I was confident as I carried the cake to church that afternoon in her metal cake carrier with a clasp-down lid. It was white with painted flowers on the outside. I carried it gingerly. The Sunday School teachers were in charge of the party, and everyone seemed to have a lot of fun.

It was about two weeks into my sixth grade school year when I was called into the office to speak with Mr. Acuff, the music teacher, however I did not know the reason. He was new to the school that year, and he had reddish hair and lots of freckles. He had a nice smile. He informed me that two instruments had been donated to the school under the condition that they would be loaned to two students who showed musical promise. He knew I could read music, and was fairly gifted in music. He said we could keep the instruments as long as we remained students at West Park Elementary. The enrollment in our elementary schools was from Kindergarten through seventh grade. After that, we transferred to Moberly Junior High.

Mr. Acuff was told to select a girl and a boy to receive either the clarinet, or the trumpet. Fifth grade was the earliest a student could be in band. He asked if I was interested, and I told him of course I was, and when asked which instrument I preferred, I told him I would prefer the clarinet. And so it was, and I was quite excited. Sam, one of my classmates, was selected and he received the trumpet. I could not wait to run home after school and tell my parents.

One of my friends played the clarinet and I was familiar enough with it, but I also knew I would need an endless supply of reeds, music books, and cork grease. I did not know how my dad would feel about the expense of these items, so my plan was to find out if I could earn extra money, by doing extra jobs for some of the women from church. I did not want anything to hinder my getting this instrument. I could now focus on another new method of broadening my love of music.

My mother had a long rectangle mirror attached to a door, so as I sat in a chair and looked into the mirror, I began to practice. The hardest part of learning to play a woodwind instrument is getting a sound out in the first place. I was careful to soak the reed in my mouth to soften the thin wood, and then carefully fit it onto the mouthpiece and tighten the band around it with the screw without breaking or splintering the reed. I prayed that I would have proper articulation, and my mouth and lower lip would fit the mouthpiece perfectly. I puckered my lips as if I was sucking on a lemon, and while doing so, made the sound "Ewe." Next, I practiced putting my flattened hand over the bottom end of the barrel, and sucked the air out of the mouthpiece as if I was drinking a milkshake. I could see and feel the lips seal around the mouthpiece and flatten my chin. It was working!

I felt ready, and I had my first beginner's book of clarinet music. I'm sure my parents grew tired of hearing me play my first song, which was, "Mary Had A little Lamb," but soon I expanded my repertoire, and was able to play many selections. The West Park Band Class played at recitals and school programs. I remained in the band through seventh grade, and then I moved on to junior high. Since I had to relinquish my instrument, I gave up being a member of band, but God would show me greater things through vocal music. God had a plan for me, even back then.

My seventh grade was very busy, but I was also making a number of new friends. At the beginning of school, our church announced that boys and girls grades six through eight could sign up for an Associational Bible Drill, but it would not take place for a few months. I wanted to participate but I did not know if I knew the chronological order of the books of the Bible well enough. I really needed to practice, so two of us partnered to try to learn together. We were each given the same kind of Bible so we would be on equal ground. We were also allowed to keep the Bibles for our own as a gift. It was such a nice King James Bible with a smooth black covering.

The orientation into the drill was explained to us in certain terms. The purpose of Youth Bible Drill was to lead us to develop skills in using our Bible. It was never to be about who was best. The skills were to locate books and verses and passages that deal with doctrinal subjects. As we worked together preparing for the drill, it increased our knowledge of the Scripture, our love for the Bible, and made us more comfortable in using the Bible to find answers to problems or questions that we, or our family and friends, might encounter.

Another benefit of the drill was to also gain poise and confidence as we answered the calls with speed and accuracy. The Youth Bible Drill was an exciting way for us to learn to use our Bibles. It was explained to us that competition wasn't what it was all about. If a young person could locate a verse quickly, learn to answer a question using Scripture, and become familiar enough with key verses we could locate from a few commands, then those teens are winners.

The leader calls the name of any book in the Bible. At the command "Start," participants began searching for the book that was called. A participant would step forward after he or she located the book and placed their index finger on any verse in the book. When called upon, the driller should be able to name that book, as well as the preceding book, and the book that follows. The leader then announces a Scripture reference to be found.

When the leader commands, "Attention," those participating must stand straight, feet together, eyes focused on the leader until they are told to "Start." The Bible is held at side in either hand, with Bible spine down, and palm supporting the back side of the Bible. The participant is taught to bring the Bible to the waistline, and to follow the command to "Present Bibles." The drill leader then announces the Scripture to be found, which was the signal for drillers to begin the search.

When located, the index finger may be placed on the actual verse called, and the person steps forward. At the end of a specified time, the timekeeper calls out the word, "Time." All drillers stop searching. The leader calls on the first driller finding the Scripture to respond. Drillers then return to their original positions, place their Bibles once again at their side, as they get ready for the next call. In our drill, the judges scored regular points and one judge scored bonus points for a job well done. The winner received a pin or a ribbon, but the real accomplishment was in knowing God's Word. By the way, I received an honorable mention.

About a year or so before the drill, my Sunday school teacher had given me a bookmark with the books of the Bible grouped into categories. I tried to learn one section at a time. There were five Books of Law from Genesis to Deuteronomy. Then there were twelve books of History from Joshua to Nehemiah. Next there were five books of Poetry and Wisdom, from Job to Song of Solomon. These were followed by seventeen books of Prophecy, containing both Major and Minor Prophets. I had to really work hard on the groups of prophets.

Next came the New Testament. I was just fine until I finished First Corinthians and Second Corinthians, then I became a bit jumbled and froze. One of the ladies at church gave me a suggestion for the next four books following both books of Corinthians. She suggested that I remember Galatians, Ephesians, Philippians and Colossians, as General Electric Power Company. I still to this day think of this as my new-found solution.

Our seventh grade class at West Park was to graduate, and as all seventh grade classes in the Moberly schools did, and a week or so before graduation we took a bus to tour the Missouri State Capitol Building in Jefferson City. I think it was always a day to which most eighth grade students looked forward. Because it was an all-day affair, and we took a sack lunch. We saw the massive Capitol Building with the large mural on the dome ceiling, and the state seal incorporated into the stone flooring of the first floor domed entryway. We visited the home of the Missouri State Governor James Blair. That was the first time I had been in Jefferson City, and viewing the Missouri River and seeing the Missouri State Penitentiary from a distance, was a huge day in itself. I was just a small town girl, in a much bigger city.

The following week, a graduation ceremony was to be held at the downtown Municipal Auditorium on a Sunday afternoon. All of the Moberly seventh grade students were to be together, and the elementary seventh grade bands would join together and perform the music we had been practicing for what seemed like months. That meant that I would be playing my clarinet for the last time. The following week I was to turn it back to the school after using it for two years. All of my many hours of practice would come to an end.

Since this was such a special event, the previous week my principal, Jenny Murphy and another one of my teachers asked if I would come to the office after school. They told me they would like to buy me a nice dress and shoes. They knew I would be playing in the band, and they saw that as something special. They measured me, and several days later, they kept me after class again and discretely handed me a bag. Inside the bag was a beautiful white dress with small bouquets of flocked flowers all over the skirt. The bodice had tucks, and was sleeveless with shoulder straps. The skirt was full, and the shoes were white leather with small spooled heels. I was speechless and I cried. They both hugged me and told me they appreciated me being an example to other kids, and a prodigy. Of course I had no idea what a prodigy meant at that time.

My sister Tib and her family had returned to Missouri for the weekend of May 18, 1958. On Sunday morning I went to church, and came home and had lunch with the family. In the late afternoon, I needed to start getting ready for the seventh grade graduation ceremony. Tib and my sister Dot began to style my hair and apply just a small amount of makeup to my face to help cover my freckled nose. Tib had purchased a pair of nylons for me, warning me to not snag them. Tib and Dot helped me dress, and looking into the mirror, I could not believe what I was seeing. I was no longer a little girl, and I was actually developing curves. I liked what I saw that day as I looked into the mirror, and when I was gathered with the other students for the concert, I received many compliments, even from some of the boys. I no longer felt like a wallflower. I felt pretty. In about three months, I would be attending school at the junior high. I was so glad my sisters were able to go to my graduation, and to also hear me play in the band.

My dad loved to go to auctions and estate sales. One Saturday during the early summer, he returned home from one such sale, and he told me that he had a surprise for me. He and my brother lifted a beautiful treadle sewing machine from his truck. I could see the word "Singer" created in the black wrought iron that curled from the base. It was very old, and it was made of walnut wood, and the head did not drop down inside the machine. There was a striking wooden box with ornate carvings matching the same rich walnut of the cabinet, and the box set down on the very top of the machine, covering the head. It was powered mechanically by a foot pedal that the person operating the machine pushed back and forth. My dad told us that he had paid seventy-five cents for this machine. That seemed unbelievable, because the machine was in perfect working order, including the belts which drove the pedal and gears.

I was delighted and my mother taught me how to sew and cut patterns. I began making most of my clothes, and I continued using this machine while both my daughters were young, before I acquired an electric machine. Learning to sew on a treadle machine would also serve to help me in my junior high Home Economics class.

EIGHT

Growth and Adjustment

WHEN I REACHED junior high, my mother and I began participating in Bible Studies through the High Noon Bible Class, under the leadership of Dr. J. Vernon McGee. He was an older Presbyterian preacher from Georgia. The broadcast later changed its name to Through the Bible Radio Broadcast, after it moved to California. They mailed us the lessons and we filled them out as we listened on our radio. He died in the late 1980s, but his teachings and radio broadcasts still live on today. I have since used many of his teaching resources in leading my own Bible Studies. I loved listening to his southern drawl as he taught.

As summer drew to an end, I was excited to finally be going to junior high. I felt so grown up. We walked from one class to the next, and we were assigned a locker. We also had a locker mate. On the first day of registration, I met a new girl whose name was Toni. She was blonde, and she was gorgeous. Her family had moved to Moberly from out of state. I had no locker mate, and neither did she. The lady behind the desk in the office asked us if we would like to share a locker, and we both agreed. I had brought a combination lock from home, and as we went to search for the exact location of the locker, I wrote down the combination to the lock and gave it to Toni.

I loved my Home Economics class. I also chose Home Economics in all four years of high school. My first teacher was Mrs. Eisenstein. We moved from sewing to child care, and then into cooking. Once a month, each of us was to prepare a baked item at home and bring it to class for her to evaluate; taste, texture, color, and presentation, along with the recipe. For this we received extra credit. Of course each girl tried to outdo the other, especially the well-regarded "teacher's pets." Yes, we did have them. It was during these years that I thought I might consider Home Economics as a career. That, of course, never took place, although as a senior, I was selected to represent our school in Kirksville, Missouri at a district home economics contest. There was nothing really hands-on, but we took tests all day and then after the testing was evaluated, we were rated and received scores based on how well we did. There were three of us that participated from our school, and we placed first in the district.

There were a certain number of electric sewing machines in our class, plus one treadle machine. There were two girls assigned to each machine, but since our class had two extra girls, Rachel Welch and I were assigned to use the treadle machine. Who could have guessed? The only problem with using this particular treadle machine was trying to regulate the length of the stitches. It was a bit different than mine. Our first project was to make an apron. Our second project was to make a skirt. Rachel was not familiar with this type of sewing machine, so I helped her as much as possible, and both our sewing projects turned out well.

Toni and I never had classes together, but it became quite apparent that she was received into the group of very popular students. She would often yell and wave to me, but she was not very neat with her part of the locker. I took the lower portion, and she the upper portion. About once a month the school conducted a locker check. The inspection was to see how orderly we kept our lockers. I purposely made sure that both portions of our locker was kept neat. Every now and then, she would tape a thank you inside our locker door. I knew why she posted it, and I was sorry if she felt guilty. I was all about being orderly and organized, which I have made my theme throughout my entire life, sometimes to a fault. She wrote in my yearbook that I was a "prodigy of many virtues." There that word was again, so I vowed to do some research as to its meaning.

Merriam-Webster explains "prodigy" as an *omen*: something *extraordinary*; an *extraordinary, marvelous, or unusual accomplishment, deed or event*; *a highly talented child or youth*. Since when does one need to have a talent to keep their locker clean?

The eighth grade, freshmen, and sophomore classes were held at the junior high school. Moberly also had a junior college, so when the junior high classes became too large, the juniors and seniors classes were moved to the junior college building, yet they were separated from the college students. They were called upper-classmen, and lower-classmen. It was a bit farther to walk to the junior college facility, but there were shortcuts that we could take without first having to go downtown.

I can't say that I really enjoyed Physical Education. Our teacher's name was Mrs. Greever. I was not the athletic person, and a bit on the pudgy side, so the only sport I could play well was Deck Tennis. I had good arm strength. During class, we wore blue cotton gym suits and the cuffed legs were so very short. We had to embroider our last name on our uniform. On the first day of the week, we had to stand on the sidelines, as Mrs. Greever came by to see if we had taken our uniform home over the weekend for laundering and ironing. Since we were required to shower after gym class, I remember standing in line and I was focused on the huge silver whistle held on a chain around her neck. I had never seen a whistle that large. She held a clipboard in her hand checking off each girl's name as she completed her shower. I was uncomfortable undressing and showering in front of the other girls. I had no sisters at home, and I was a very private person.

As ninth graders, we were also introduced to the dances that were held once every three months. The dances were called Jamborees, and they were held during the evening. Many of the girls were taller than the boys, and watching them dance together made me chuckle to myself. We had known about these dances when we were in eighth grade, and we were quite excited to finally be able to experience them. The teachers chaperoned, and no one outside of the school could attend. They lasted for about two hours, and we were served cookies and punch. I didn't know if my dad would allow me to attend, so I talked to my brother.

My brother Mick was a sophomore, and he was beginning to notice girls. I know this, because one day while going through the lunch line, he was looking at a girl, and stuck his hand in the butter. Of course I never let him forget that moment. I was also jealous of my brother. I did not care for some of the girls that he liked, and I didn't think they were good enough for him. With a reversal of roles, he thought the same thing about this little sister. He made me walk through dance steps with him while our dad was gone. I knew the steps, but I had my doubts that I would be asked to dance anyway, and I surely didn't want to dance with my brother.

I asked Mick if he would talk to our dad and put in a good word, giving me permission to attend the dance. Although Mick was very protective of me, he also advised our parents about certain kids with whom he didn't think I should associate. Our dad trusted his advice, and when Mick explained that it was more of a school party than a dance, our dad gave in and allowed me to attend the parties. After that, we were careful to not call them dances. Jimmy Phipps lived across the street from us, and he was in my class. Jimmy's mother was a friend of my parents who normally drove Jimmy to various functions. She agreed that I could go with them. She drove us to school, and returned to pick us up when the dance was over. A friend of Mick owned a car, so he and a few others rode with him to the dance.

My dad was quite strict with me. I'm not sure if it was because some my older sisters had left home or gotten married at such young ages, or if he was just overly protective of his youngest daughter. Since I was the last child, I think he was trying to hold on, but the reins sometimes felt too snug. He had remarked that I could not date until I was sixteen, and in fact, some of my sisters married at that same age. My mother knew how I felt, and yet I did not develop a rebellious attitude, argue my case, nor disrespect my parents. I do not think he had a thing to worry about, because none of the boys had noticed me anyway. To them, I was overly bookish, and a church goer, and that was not what the majority of them was looking for in a girl.

I jumped head first into my studies, but music was becoming even more important in my life. Mrs. Claudine Triplett was my music teacher, and she was a jewel. She recognized my talent and was willing to work with me to train my voice. My brother, Mick, had also been her student. He told me that she was his first love. I smiled because she was an older woman. She called him "Dimples," and she also selected him to play special parts in a number of musical roles. I call it doting on him, but he did have talent.

For our junior high school Christmas program in 1959, a trio was formed to sing a particular music selection, which was "The Birthday of a King." Those who were chosen for the trio were all named Barbara, including Barbara Maxey, Barbara Ricky and me. Subsequently, we were referred to as the three Barbaras. At this time, we were still under the direction of Mrs. Triplett.

Mrs. Triplett first served as supervisor of vocal education in the entire Moberly school system. After three years the program was expanded, and she was named supervisor of vocal music in the secondary schools as well. Under her direction, Moberly High School and Junior College were consistently represented by outstanding vocal groups. She was a great teacher. She was, however, criticized for requiring the girls in the higher grades to wear formals for a special performance at least once a year, and some could not afford them.

Mrs. Triplett organized the Mojuco Singers, which each year consists of 30 select voices chosen in auditions at the start of the term. The actual name was MOJUCO, an acronym for Moberly Junior College Singers. The members were made up of high school juniors and seniors, as well as those in the two years of junior college. I would later be a part of this group. The Mojuco Singers presented concerts in many states and institutions. I have fond memories of fund-raisers, car washes, selling homemade candy, and selling hot dogs and soft drinks at the sporting events in an effort to finance our spring tour. Mrs. Triplett resigned to be on staff at Kirksville State Teacher's College, and Neil Zumwalt became our vocal music instructor, and was there for the remainder of my time as a student in Moberly. I became very close with both Mr. Zumwalt and his wife. One might say, they sort of took me under their wings.

At church, I was asked to sing in ensembles, and occasionally I sang a solo. I always felt that God was somehow guiding me into music. Our choir director noticed that I had selected "Stranger of Galilee" as a solo. She began to chuckle. I didn't know why she was laughing until she shared a story with me. Her father was a minister, and he wore dentures. One Sunday, he sang this song as a solo. While he was singing, he lost his upper teeth. They landed on the podium, and he acted as if nothing had happened, quickly picking them up, and putting them into the pocket of his trousers.

My freshman year seemed to go by so fast, and soon the school year would end. My sister Tib invited me to come to Minnesota to spend the summer and babysit for them. They had a three month old baby girl, Patty, and now it was time for Tib to return to work from maternity leave. They also had two other children, Deb and Steven. Deb was six and

Steven was three. My parents were a little reluctant, but finally gave in to this request. I had just turned 15 years old, but I was very responsible. Tib would be paying me for babysitting, and I could save the money.

I thought about this offer for over a month. Not only would I miss my parents, but I would also miss my friends and church family that truly did feel like family. My parents would be alone because Mick was considering enlisting in the US Army, even though our parents would have to sign permission for him to enlist. At that time he was not yet of legal age. I surely would miss him. As I grew in my faith, I prayed about this matter a lot.

The day arrived when I packed my belongings and said a temporary goodbye to my parents with a full intention of coming back home within the three month time frame. I sensed that my mother was particularly sad, almost as if she could sense that something would change. The next morning as I slid into the back seat of my brother-in-law and sister's newer turquoise and white 1957 Chevy Bel Air, we began our journey north.

I had never before been this far from home. It was going to be a new experience, but I was hopeful that it would be a positive one. I watched as the city turned into country, and as we drove through Iowa, there seemed to be one farm after another for mile after mile. The fields of corn were already a foot or so tall, just enough to begin to bend in the wind. I noticed that the corn also seemed to be such a rich dark color of green. My dad had told me that was how you could tell it had been fertilized.

The interstate system had not yet been built through this part of Iowa, so the maximum speed while driving a vehicle, was much lower than it is today. I played games with Deb and Steven in the back seat, and I read Burma Shave signs. We stopped for lunch at a truck stop in Waterloo, Iowa. I was told they normally stopped at this same place to eat, when travelling to and from Moberly.

It was early evening when we arrived at their home in South Saint Paul. They lived in a huge two story farm house with an extremely long driveway off the main highway. They rented the house from a farmer who still used the land to plant crops and raise cattle. Could I have known I would indeed walk this driveway in deep snow later that very winter? For now, I was surprised to see puddles of water in the gravel driveway that were still frozen. This was the end of May and yet there was still ice? This was so different from Missouri.

It was very true that the Minnesota summers were much cooler than Missouri summers. It did not actually start warming up until after the first of June. The growing season for garden vegetables was also short. The sunny days and cool nights were perfect for tomatoes; however the growth and maturity didn't last very many weeks, nevertheless it was great for cabbage and potatoes.

Once settled, one of the first things that I did was to search for a Baptist church to attend. A friend of my sister's family recommended a church, which I visited the next Sunday. My sister drove me and picked me up afterward. My sister and brother-in-law were themselves of the Catholic faith, but it was important to her that I attended a church of my own faith.

I fell in love with the people at church, and the teenagers were so sweet and friendly. Every few Sundays, the choir was made up of the youth, which meant that every few weeks the youth had choir practice on Wednesday night. I had never seen so many teenagers and young college kids participating in church activities. On Wednesday evening, the Erickson family picked me up and took me home. They had a teenage daughter as well as a teenage son. Their daughter was sweet, and their son was really cute. They lived in South Saint Paul, not far from the area where my sister lived, however a bit closer to town. It was not an inconvenience for them to pick me up, but even if it had been, they were kind and generous people and would never have said it was problematic.

I took care of my nieces and nephew over the summer, becoming greatly attached to them. I played outside with Deb and Steven if Patty was sleeping. The windows were open, so I could listen for her. If she was awake, I took her outside in her stroller and kept her close to me. The summer temperatures were very mild. We sat on the front porch and watched the gophers at work in the huge front yard. I had never seen a gopher, and although Minnesota is known as the gopher state, it was not the state's official symbol. Deb and I often went into Saint Paul or Minneapolis on Saturday afternoon to see a movie, and before going to the movie theater, we had lunch at a Woolworth close by. Tib dropped us off, and picked us up when the movie was over. The normal thing for Deb to order for lunch was chicken noodle soup and a grilled cheese sandwich, and that never changed.

That summer was the first time I had experienced a state fair. The Minnesota State Fair was held in August, in Saint Paul's Como Park. Even at fifteen, I was awestruck. There were so many people, so many rides, so many games, so much food, and so much music. We spent the entire day, and into late evening. We rode the Ferris wheel, the roller coaster, and any other exciting ride. Our friend's son, Robbie, was with us, and even though he was a year younger than me, as the kids today often say, we were crushing on one another.

The summer was drawing to a close. I became confused over a choice of whether I wanted to return home or not. Telephone calls were expensive, so I did not talk to my parents very often. My mother and I wrote back and forth once a week, and I could sense the loneliness on every page of her letter. I knew however, that my parents had very little, and if I did return home, once again they would be burdened with the additional expense for my care. I decided to talk to Tib.

We discussed my staying there for the school year and caring for the children. On the flip-side, I wanted to go to school. I decided I would do both. I would remain there, and also do home schooling. I paid for that myself. I was very much attached to my nieces and nephew. I proudly showed them off to my friends and girlfriends every chance I could when Tib drove me to church. At home I tied a towel around Patty's waist and worked with her as she learned to stand.

In August, I broke the news to my parents that I wanted to stay. They didn't say much, but we promised that we would come home for Thanksgiving, and when the school year was over, I would be home for good. Ted's mother had already agreed when school was over for the year, she would then move to Minnesota and live with them and care for her grandchildren. I think my parent's reluctance was entertaining the possibility that I wouldn't return home at all, but that I might meet someone and get married and live in Minnesota like my sister Julie had done years earlier when she went to live with Tib.

Deb was in the first grade, and she rode the bus. Each morning I got her ready for school, fed her breakfast, and walked her to the bus. When I returned, it was time to get Steven up, and wake Patty for her breakfast and bath time. After my chores were done, I did my school work as I settled down with the children around me for the day. When I was finished with my curriculum, I mailed it and awaited the school to respond with my grades.

I spent some of the weekends with my brother Charles and his family in Cottage Grove, as well as my sister Julie and her family in Minneapolis. I also spent a few weekends with Ted's brother Joe, and his wife Louise, in South Saint Paul. Joe and Louise had a baby that was sight impaired, and legally blind. Her name is Jackie, and at that time, she would not allow very many people to hold her and take care of her. Since I very much had the same body build as her mother, and I also had long hair, she did not fuss when I cared for her. She felt of my face and my hair. Babies are smart, and they can feel things. It was difficult for Joe and Louise to find a babysitter for that reason. It was a treat for them when I spent the weekend, which allowed them to actually have a date. They lived near the church that I attended, and one of them always drove me to service on Sunday morning.

By Halloween it had turned cold, and the snow began to fall. I knew how cold Missouri could get, and if Minnesota was colder, then I was in for a massive experience. There were some enormous snows that winter, but even though the temperatures reached 30 below, and the snow became deep, the cold was different than it was in Missouri. The house was heated with fuel oil, a smaller stove in the kitchen and utility room, and a larger stove in the living room area, with bedrooms leading off to both sides. We lived on the main floor, but the bathroom was upstairs. There was a grate opening in the ceiling, above the stove in the living room, which allowed heat to rise to the main room upstairs plus the bathroom.

One particular Saturday, both Tib and Ted were scheduled to work. They were employed by Armour's Meat Packing Company. Deb had Catechism on Saturday morning, so she rode the bus to church and back home. I always walked with her down the driveway to see that she reached the bus safely. It wasn't long before it began snowing, and then turned into blizzard conditions. Toward mid-morning I received a call from the church informing me that the bus could not make the return trip. I told the caller that I would call Deb's parents and give them the message, so just keep her there until they got off work.

When my sister and brother-in-law arrived at the rectory, Monsignor had invited Deb to have lunch with him. The sisters had prepared chicken noodle soup, which was Deb's very favorite. He later shared with Deb's parents, that as she was eating the soup, and seemed to be enjoying it, she said to him, "Your wife sure is a good cooker." Deb was never shy, but she certainly did love chicken noodle soup.

That winter, Mick actually did join the US Army, so when we went home for a visit at Thanksgiving, he was gone. Shortly afterward, he graduated from Boot Camp and was sent to Germany for a year. He began sending money home to our folks, and the next spring they had an inside bathroom built. The visit served to be good not only for my parents, but also for me. I did not go see my friends while I was home because I wanted to spend every minute with my mom and dad before going back to Minnesota. I had to also gather my winter clothing and coats to take back to South Saint Paul with me.

In January, the church I was attending in South Saint Paul organized a youth retreat. We took two buses and went to White Bear Lake Resort for the weekend. There were youth from other churches who were also there at the lodge. Two people shared a room, and we had Bible Study, speakers, testimonies from some of the young people, good food, and indoor activities, along with many out-of-door winter activities. It proved to be an amazing weekend.

The remainder of the winter was uneventful, and a typical Minnesota winter to spring, which was long, cold, and snowy. Ted and his friends went deer hunting, and after skinning the deer, and removing the meat from the carcass, they cut it up and packaged the meat. Several of Ted's friends were butchers at Armours Meat Packing plant where they worked together. I helped to wrap and label the packages of venison.

I took the opportunity to explore the upstairs part of the farm house that winter. I loved to clean and organize, so I sorted through junk and I threw away a number of things that had been left in the house by a former tenant. There was nothing valuable, so I took it down to the barn and put everything in barrels so that it could be discarded in the spring. I cleaned the rooms and scrubbed the floors until the hardwood shined. Now Deb and Steven could play upstairs. There were sixteen rooms in the farm house, plus an attic entrance off the kitchen, which I also investigated, finding nothing of importance.

NINE

Going Home

THE SCHOOL YEAR was ended, and I was ready to return home. The year was 1961, and I had just turned 16. The year had been long, and I had grown and matured in ways that I did not think possible, especially my faith. Being around the group of young people at church was amazing. Their faith was real. The main thing that I was ready to do, was to get back to my parents, my friends, my church, and my music. Before we were to leave, one of the girls from youth group called me to invite me to her home for dinner as a final time to be together. My sister, who obviously knew what she was planning, drove me to her house and when I went inside, some of the youth were hiding in another room. Unbeknownst to me, they all yelled, "Surprise," as they jumped out of hiding.

As a going away gift, my friends gave me a large stuffed Dalmatian, as well as other gifts. The Walt Disney movie *101 Dalmatians* had been released a few months before, and a few of us had gone to see the movie. We ate sandwiches, snacks, cake, and punch, and just enjoyed a good time together one last time. As we parted and shared hugs, I thanked them for making me feel so welcome in their group that past year, and we vowed to correspond. We were faithful to write to one another through the course of several years.

Two days later we packed my belongings and drove south. I was certainly taking more home than I had brought with me when I arrived one year ago. During the final few miles, especially when we drove into my home town, a calm feeling washed over me. I didn't realize just how homesick I actually was. Within a few days I was unpacked, and it was so good to finally have indoor plumbing. Living in Minnesota had spoiled me. Mick was still gone, so I moved into his room.

Our neighbor owned Brook's Café, a downtown restaurant. Opal's husband, Vincil, had a small one-man taxi service. Opal asked if I would like to come to work for her. She paid 50 cents an hour, and the job would be working in the kitchen, washing dishes and helping her cook. There was no automatic dishwasher, so the dishes had to be washed by hand. Even though it was during the summer, and there was no air conditioning in the back part, I didn't mind. I have always found washing dishes to be relaxing. She also taught me how to grill steaks and hamburger, make slaw with a clear dressing, peel fresh potatoes to be cut into fries, make meringue for pies, and how to pound out the meat to be used for hand bread tenderloins.

Since I worked in the back part of the kitchen, I often saw black men come through the alley by way of the back door. I didn't understand why they sat down at a table in back room, but Opal went to the back and took their order. I always gave them a kind word, and I cleaned the table after they left, but none of them replied. I felt sorry for each of these men.

You see, in my town, the civil rights movement had not yet taken place. Just because our schools had been integrated, did not mean that a black and a white could sit at the same table together. Neither was a black man supposed to speak to a white woman. My heart ached. My parents had taught me as a young child to respect everyone, no matter their race. I had heard testimonials from my dad concerning the black men that he had worked alongside, sat down and shared lunch together, and probably had swigged out of the same wine or whiskey bottle and shot craps together. My parents taught us to never disrespect anyone.

I worked at the café for the rest of the summer. The money that I earned enabled me to purchase fabric and other necessities for the next school year. It was time to go to school and register for the next year. I walked into the school office at the Moberly Junior High School, thinking I was going to be a junior, only to be told that none of the subjects I had taken while living in Minnesota would be accepted or applied as credits toward my graduation in Missouri. Because of this, my tenth grade would have to be repeated. I was devastated. I would not be in the same class as all of my previous classmates. I would not be rejoining them. I would not be graduating with them in 1963. I would instead have to wait until 1964, and I would be 19 years of age.

I registered, and chose the classes that I needed. I was given my schedule, and my locker number. I felt dejected, and it really didn't matter this time if I had a locker with someone of my choosing, or have someone assigned to share my locker. I felt crushed. The next few days were overwhelmingly gloomy, but there was nothing I could do about it. By now, I had learned in my spiritual journey, to lean on some of the instructions given us in the Bible. One of these verses from Proverbs 16:9 NIV reads, "*A man's heart plans his way, but the Lord directs his steps.*" I was convinced that God still had a plan, even though I certainly didn't know what it was.

Through the summer I had made new friends, especially a few new ones at church. I met a really nice girl my age who was spending the summer with her aunt and uncle. Her name was Marva Behnke. Her uncle was one of our church deacons, and she lived in Milwaukee, Wisconsin. Our older youth group began to engage in biblical theology discussing passages of Scripture, and we also began to study different faiths and beliefs. I was very much interested in this type of study. Marva was from a different faith, but she began attending, and she began asking me a great number of questions. By the end of summer, she embraced the Southern Baptist faith, accepted Jesus as her personal Savior, and asked Pastor Jimmy if he would baptize her by immersion. She convinced her parents that this was a choice she wanted to make. She and I remained close for a number of years, keeping in touch through letters.

By the time school began, I was upbeat. I went holding my head high, resigned to the fact there was nothing I could do about the situation. Of course my close friends knew the reason since I had shared it with them, but I was determined to make the best of a bad situation.

I recall a young girl who enrolled at our high school having moved from Oklahoma. Her name was Charlotte, and she was Native American. She had bronze skin and coal black hair. My niece, Susie, and I took her to lunch at the restaurant where I had worked that summer. Opal called me aside to speak with me personally. She informed me that a black person could not be served in the restaurant. I politely made it known to her that our friend's heritage was Native American, and not Black. That seemed to satisfy her, but it made me so sad, because this was such an injustice no matter the race, and it was such a shame that mankind could pick and choose who could be welcomed and served, and who could not.

The best thing to happen, was for me to meet Mr. Zumwalt. Not only was he our music teacher, he was also the director of Mojuco Singers at Moberly Junior College. He began choosing individuals and forming solos, duets, trios, quartets, and sextets for junior high. He even arranged a triple-trio. He simply asked each of us to sing for him and to sight read music scores. I became a part of several of these groups. He also directed the Glee Clubs, both male and female. Since God had given me a heart for music, I embraced each of these opportunities, and I had learned that every good and perfect gift comes from the Lord. After returning home, I was also singing more frequently at church.

At home, I helped my mother organize, and I helped her sew new curtains as we did some rearranging. My dad built two more rooms on the back part of the house after he bought it, and since I was now using my brother's room as my own, what used to be my bedroom was now a closet and a bathroom, which I helped my mother decorate. From my first year as a teenager, I had a hope chest. It really wasn't a chest. It was, in fact, a large round heavy cardboard can with a lid. Aunt Lillie had given it to me, and she called it a paper barrel. Every now and then someone gave me a gift, and I stored it in the barrel to save it for the time when I would either live by myself or get married. I had several sets of sheets, towels, and some cookware that a friend had given me when she bought a new set. The barrel also contained promotional items that were inside boxes of detergent and Quaker Oats and a few other items that my mother had given me.

In the 1950s, Duz Detergent made buyers happy by including a piece of Golden Wheat Dinnerware in each box of their laundry soap. There were platters, dinner plates, salad plates and bread & butter plates. Around 1960, the year before I returned home from Minnesota, they began putting soup bowls, berry bowls, vegetable bowls and cups with saucers in the boxes. Soon after that, there were sugars, creamers and gravy boats. There were clear glass coordinated juice glasses and tumblers. My mother began collecting some of these items for me.

There were hand towels inside the detergent. It depended on the promotional date of purchase, and the size of the box as to the contents of the box. The marketing item changed now and then. The company began this promotion to gain sales over Tide detergent. Each month an extra plate, bowl or serving piece was added to the boxes of Duz to entice customers to buy the soap in order to acquire the dinnerware. If someone needed one of the pieces, women would trade for something they needed. Also in the 1960s, the Quaker Oats Company offered Anchor Hocking glassware pieces in boxes of their oatmeal. The glassware featured a starburst design and is often referred to as the oatmeal pattern. These pieces were manufactured for mass home distribution. They include: a berry bowl, a punch cup, saucers, a sherbet or custard bowl, a soap dish, a juice tumbler, a short tumbler and a water tumbler. My mother had many of these pieces.

I remember being so delighted to find the new prize inside each time we opened the oatmeal box. Of course my father ate oatmeal every morning of the week, so we purchased a lot of oatmeal. The pieces were quite durable.

My dad had picked up a small desk for me at an auction. While I was living in Minnesota, I had purchased a small, square AM radio. I found the perfect spot for it on the desk, where I could listen as I did my homework. There was a really great radio station in Kansas City, and soon I began listening to WHB, for which the acronym was labeled, "World's Happiest Broadcasters." For most of the 1960s and 1970s, WHB was one of the nation's most influential Top 40 outlets. The station later moved to a different frequency. As I sat at my desk every night doing my homework, I listened to the top forty songs which were the most popular tunes of that day. I kept the volume low, so as to not disturb my parents who were definitely glued to a western movie on their television.

The bizarre thing was my typing class. I just could not keep my fingers in a position that was solid enough to reach the keys of the typewriter. Most of us had manual typewriters, but the school had also purchased a few electric machines. Within the first two weeks of school, we were given the chance to switch classes if we had a problem. I had always been near the top of the class academically, but I was afraid that my typing was so bad it was going to keep me from being on the Honor Roll. I dropped typing, but still kept shorthand. Mr. Edwards taught shorthand, and he allowed me to transpose my shorthand by writing longhand. In spite of this, I could still take dictation at 120 words per minute, and 90 words per minute for five minutes straight.

Surprisingly, I was still on the Honor Roll. I did think my decision to drop typing was rather silly, because if I had a job in which I had to take dictation, but yet I couldn't type, what good would it do me? I did well in all of my classes, and I was able to take four solids most years, along with several electives. I carried a full load through school without a Study Hall, which meant that I had homework every night.

The musical groups at school under the direction of Neil Zumwalt, were often invited to sing before local groups such as the Ministerial Alliance, Kiwanis Club, Rotary Club, and also men's and women's social groups. We wore matching attire, usually black and white, and the girls wore a red bow around the collar. The boys wore red ties. These standard uniforms could be mixed in with any of the groups. I was part of a duet, trio, and sextet, so we were pretty much settled in the area of costume, without having to change clothing during performances. I made my own black skirts. Both Glee Clubs performed at larger functions, such as school programs. The clothing we wore for these was more the traditional clothing, and did not have to match others. Mr. Zumwalt called these our "church" clothes.

The school year came to a close, my second year as a tenth-grader was over, and it was 1962. I could now begin the next year as a junior at the Moberly Junior College. I had been working part-time at the local Ben Franklin. I worked only a short amount of time that summer, and then the person I was replacing returned to work, and I was let go. Several months prior, I had celebrated my seventeenth birthday, but I still did not have the desire to learn to drive. I had nothing to drive anyway.

As I worked the candy counter, I got sick of looking

at the candy. I stood behind the counter with glassed-in sections that separated the different candies, and I weighed the candy, bagged it for the customers, and took their money. I waited patiently for children to select which kind of candy they wanted as they looked at the amount of money they were holding in the palm of their hand. They looked at the candy, and then at the money, back and forth, and often I tried to help them make up their minds. I remembered just a few years back when I did the same thing while bearing my only treasured nickel, standing in front of the candy counter at Sam May's Grocery at the west end of Collins Avenue. "Let's see, should I get jawbreakers, BB Bats, or Tootsie Rolls?" It was known as "penny candy," but sometimes you could get two or more pieces for a penny. It seemed so long ago that I was that skinny, straight haired, shy little girl.

I spent a great deal of time that summer in Independence, Missouri with my sister and her husband. Mary and Bob had four young daughters. I rode the train to Kansas City and they picked me up at Union Station. That was a huge place. I discovered that Mary and Bob's house was in Kentucky Hills. I had heard the commercial for this development on the Kansas City radio station, WHB. I thought it was the prettiest house ever. The commercial said, "Kentucky Hills, the most peaceful place in greater Kansas City."

There were a number of teenage girls in their neighborhood and we became acquainted. We had sleep-overs at one another's homes. They tried to talk me into playing with an Ouija Board, but I told them it was evil. I really did have a great time while I was there, and I especially loved my nieces. I sat on the front steps at night, and I looked out at all of the lights sprinkled over the city, and I thought it was amazing. When I lived in Minnesota we lived on a farm, so this was my first time of experiencing so many lights.

Bob had a Jeep, and he had established an ice-cream route for that summer. He hired Ronnie, a teenager from their neighborhood to help him with the route, which left himself free to drive the vehicle. I think Ronnie must have eaten up a lot of Bob's profit. There was always a storehouse of ice-cream and Bomb-Pops in the basement freezer at home.

My sister introduced me to the Montgomery Ward and the Sears outlets in Kansas City. She was good at finding a bargain, and if she saw something that she thought I could use, and she thought I would like it, she usually bought it for me. I was so appreciative.

During this particular summer, my sister found out she was expecting their fifth child. She and I sewed several maternity dresses. I remember one of them was made of a brown and white checked gingham fabric. At least she had an electric sewing machine. I thought about making a new dress myself, but we were running out of time, and I had to go home before school began. The sack, chemise, and balloon style dresses were popular, along with pill-box hats, thanks to Jacqueline Kennedy.

When the summer break ended and I had returned home, my girlfriends and I would sometimes gather to hang out on Saturday. Most of their homes were large, and many had an upstairs. I had always dreamed of an upstairs bedroom. Most of them were near the downtown area, which was the nicer area of town. The homes in those areas had beautiful front doors, and a cement front porch that spanned much of the width of the house. Some had porch swings and brick columns. They were nothing like the house in which I lived. I think that is the reason I did not invite my friends to my home. It was still a small house with rolled siding on the outside, that looked like brick, but really wasn't. Through the years, God was going to teach me that the outside it is not what matters, but what is on the inside that really counts. I think it bothered me more than it bothered anyone else. Our home was always neat and tidy. As I grew older, I was convicted for comparing material things, knowing that was not important, but quite often that is the mindset of an immature person. I learned that we must always be thankful for the things that we have, instead of wishing for the things that we do not have.

I now had a little few extra dollars from an occasional babysitting job, so I could afford to stop at the drug store for a Coke now and then, and perhaps even go to a movie. My girlfriends and I strolled along the downtown streets while window shopping, and my favorite store was P.N. Hirsh. Let's step back in time and go shoe shopping in downtown Moberly. There were most likely shoe departments at J.C. Penney's, which by the way, the Moberly establishment was the first J.C. Penney to exist in Missouri. Montgomery Ward probably had a shoe department, but P.N. Hirsh not only had stylish shoes to fit me, but they were also less expensive that the other stores.

When I was younger, my dad often talked about one of his friends, and then he laughed as he shared the tremendous size of his friend's feet. Once someone asked my dad how big his friend's feet were, and he said, "He wears a size 13," and then he laughed again. He said the man's feet were so big, they wouldn't fit into the wash pan.

In my immature mind, size 13 must have been huge if it

made my dad laugh. When my dad took me to P.N. Hirsh to be fitted for shoes before the beginning of school, the shoe salesman looked carefully at the shoes I was wearing, and said to my dad, "Well, her feet have grown this year, so now she will need a size 13."

I remember bursting into tears, thinking that now I was going to be wearing a size 13, and everyone would laugh at me like they laughed at my dad's friend. My dad didn't know what was wrong, and I didn't tell him. Of course I was unaware that an adult size 13 was in a different category than a child's size 13. I was, however, gifted with large feet. Nobody ever passed down their hand-me-down shoes, because they were always too small. I wear a size 10, and have always been self-conscious of the size of my feet. I later stated, that if God had not created my feet so large, I would probably have been taller.

Reed Street was like a big outdoor mall with dozens of retail stores, and most of them were locally owned. Of course these stores either went out of business or have relocated to other parts of town. When I was growing up, the store hours along Reed Street were typically nine to five on Monday through Friday, nine to nine on Saturday; and closed on Sunday. In the five-hundred block of West Reed, there was Patterson's Department Store.

When I was in the ninth grade, a trench coat was a must. Every girl had a trench coat from Patterson's. I guess I moaned about it for so long, my dad told me to meet him there one day during lunch. The only color I could find to fit, was in a sage green, and it had a lightweight lining. He bought it for me, and I stopped begging, but as I look back to those days, I can see how very selfish I was, because my dad did not have that kind of money to spend on something I wanted, instead of something I needed. The really sad thing was that within that next month, I caught the pocket on a door knob, ripping the fabric. My mother did her best to repair the coat, but every time I looked at it, I felt a thorn in my flesh as I remembered that I just could not live without a trench coat.

That summer was the best one that I could remember personally, but my dad's health also began to fail. He suffered a mini-stroke, which is also what I now know to be a TIA, or in other words, a Transient Ischemic Attack. This is a temporary period of symptoms, similar to those of a stroke. A TIA usually lasts only a few minutes and does not cause permanent damage, however it may be a warning sign that something might perhaps lead to a stroke within a few months. My dad was around 64 years of age, and he had begun receiving Social Security benefits, which really was not much money every month. He was also receiving a small allotment each month from the Veterans' Administration as a benefit for having lost a lung in WWI, but it too, was small. I tried to spare my parents as much expense as possible, although I knew they would do as much as they could for me.

Our dad had some health concerns several years prior to this, and during that time, Mick voluntarily went to work in the hay field, earning enough money to sustain us through the summer. He was around 14 or 15 years of age, and he kept no money for himself, except to buy several pairs of blue jeans for school in the fall. I will forever be grateful for my brother stepping up unselfishly, to help sustain us.

TEN

A Song in My Heart

IN 1962, DURING my first week as a junior, Mr. Zumwalt sent out a notice that there would be auditions for anyone wanting to join the Mojuco Singers. They needed to fill several spots left vacant by graduates of both high school seniors, as well as junior college graduates. Once a member, the student was locked in for the remaining number of years they were enrolled. The group consisted of 30 members. He sent me a private message to be sure to try out. I was selected and it became a sort of roller coaster from that point.

We assembled at the junior college at seven o'clock each morning during the school week, where we practiced for one hour before going to our first class. I appreciate my dad for making sure I arrived each day without being late. He no longer drove on the highway, but he did drive short distances to town and back home. He told me he was proud of me, and I was a good girl. We did not receive credit hours for being in this group, but the very satisfaction was more than enough to compensate. We worked together as a group earning money for our spring tour, to help fund our travel to other states to perform. Mr. Zumwalt always arranged our performances, and since he had arranged several different stops, he often used different programs at various stops. Each program was different than the preceding one, also using different arrangements and vocals. He planned some of the performances to be conducted at major churches and schools throughout the states. This often allowed the group to spend the night in the school's empty dorms. Many times the school would include breakfast as an added bonus.

Each female in the choir was responsible for sewing her own dress, or having someone else make the dress. We chose the pattern and selected the fabric. The dress was black and the form was a straight-line. We wore black heels, white gloves, and white pearl beads with clip-on earrings to match the necklace. Each of these items were identical, and they were purchased from Patterson's Department Store. I used my own money to purchase these items, sparing my dad the expense. We looked nice and uniform. The boys wore white shirts, white jackets, black slacks, black shoes and black ties. We were scheduled often to perform at various local functions, and several times each year we gave a concert at the Moberly Municipal Auditorium with a ticket price of 75 cents. This was what we called a dress rehearsal in preparation for the spring tour. We learned useful skills by performing in public before a large audience, making sure we were confident before we left on the spring tour.

The junior year was not altogether fun and games. We had to work especially hard to make sure our academics were kept up. I did not have a job, but I was frequently asked to babysit. Fortunately I was able to stay on task, and managed quite well, but I often had to let my social life suffer as a result.

Somewhere around the last of October, Mr. Zumwalt called me aside and asked if I would help him out by singing in a cantata that he was directing at First Christian Church of Madison, Missouri. The small town of Madison was about fifteen miles north of Moberly. He was the music and choir director at the church. There were 20 or so middle age to older folks in the choir, so he was thinking if he could enlist two of his students from Mojuco Singers, it would greatly help with the cantata. Dale Sivert, a gifted tenor, accepted the offer, and I agreed to sing as well.

We practiced each Wednesday evening. Mr. Zumwalt and his wife, along with Dale, came to pick me up at my house. Mrs. Zumwalt was also part of the church choir. As I said before, I was not very proud of the house in which I lived, but neither Mr. Zumwalt nor Mrs. Zumwalt treated me any less than respectful. I believe this helped me overcome my anxiety over this matter. The choir members were so appreciative of our help. In fact, Dale and I were asked in advance if we could also assist them with their Easter cantata in the spring. On both occasions following the cantata, the choir took us out to eat at Reed's Corner Restaurant in Moberly.

It was during this year that I began dating. I didn't date Moberly boys, but I did date several who were from the surrounding towns. Most of these began as blind dates, which were set up by my girlfriends. Virginia Mehlfeld was mostly responsible for the blind dates. With school, church activities, and music groups, I didn't really have a lot of time for dating.

I became good friends with several classmates, and I remember Yonnie Bell and Janie Kehoe inviting me to eat lunch with them on the outside lawn. I sat beside Yonnie during music class and Mr. Zumwalt called each of us up in front of the class to sing a portion of a music arrangement as part of our grade. If the student needed help, he allowed them to choose someone to sing with them, and Yonnie usually chose me to sing with her.

Those of us who belonged to the Mojuco Singers were truly busy learning our music, because we never used sheet music. When we sang, it was totally from memorization. We had only a few months remaining before we were to leave on the tour. After our Christmas break, we discussed and voted as to where we wanted to go. The goal was to go to some place the group had never before been. We chose to go to Illinois by way of Saint Louis, and travel south through Kentucky and Tennessee, to the Great Smoky Mountains. After deciding, Mr. Zumwalt planned and made our scheduled stops.

Mr. Zumwalt reported that our first stop was to sing at a high school in Saint James, and then to Farmington, Missouri, for a concert, and another performance at a senior citizen's home. We would end with a concert at a Presbyterian children's home in Saint James, Missouri, where we would be rewarded with dinner and rooms for the night.

The next stop would be to perform at Fredericktown, cross over the Mississippi River at Cape Girardeau, into Illinois and Kentucky and down into Nashville. Before crossing into Illinois, we would have dinner on a riverboat, just for the experience. While in Nashville, we were scheduled to visit the Hermitage Plantation and Museum, home of Andrew Jackson. We were planning to spend several nights at the historic downtown Hermitage Hotel. From there we would go to Chattanooga and see the Great Smoky Mountains. We planned to spend several days of sight-seeing, ending with Easter Sunday services, followed by a trip to Lookout Mountain. We would return to Nashville for the night, before returning home the next day.

We worked hard earning money with every fundraiser possible, along with cleaning the inside and outside of vehicles for donations. We also picked up and delivered the vehicles. Of course whenever we sang at local luncheons, the Rotary Club, Kiwanis Club, or other groups, we were given donations that also helped to fund the trip. We were also to charter a bus for the trip.

While a Mojuco Singers member, I grew especially close to a particular group of students who attended Union Avenue Christian Church in Moberly, so I began attending their church. There were seven of us who were members of the 30 member group of the singers. Raymond Gibson was the pastor, but he was also one of the Moberly pastors who served at a correctional facility. This was the Missouri Department of Corrections facility, a state prison for both medium and minimum-security prisoners. He also taught a class at the junior college. He and Mr. Zumwalt often arranged for the Mojuco Singers to attend a Sunday morning worship service with the inmates at the facility, and present several songs. On occasion, the prison choir would sing in addition to our group. The name of their choir was "The Prodigals." They were amazing. The first time we visited the prison it was quite a strange feeling to hear the sound of iron gates close behind us. We did not know what to expect, but once we were in the same area with the inmates, none of them appeared intimidating.

My sister in Independence was close to giving birth to child number five. My teachers granted me a week off so I could go and be with her. They each assigned my homework. I arrived on the train one day, and three days later on January 22nd, 1963, the baby was born, another sweet baby girl. I stayed for the week, and went home the following weekend.

In the weeks leading up to our tour, several of my sisters and brothers sent money for me to use for incidental items on our trip. I was grateful for their gifts, and humbled to say the least. The weeks progressed into spring, and soon it was time for the Mojuco Singers to leave on tour. While gathered at the chartered bus to board, Mr. and Mrs. Zumwalt called me aside. Very diplomatically, they asked me if I had money to spend. I told them that I did, and that my siblings had provided it. My heart was full, because of the compassion they showed. This is one of the reasons that I respected them so much. There was extra money left from our fundraisers, and it was divided equally and put into envelopes, one for each member. This was money left from the expenses incurred with the trip, such as the chartered bus, hotel, meals, and meals. We were all grateful to have the extra money.

Our first stop was to have lunch in Saint Louis. The bus was very comfortable with plenty of room to stretch out. We made stops every few hours for bathroom breaks and snacks. During the travel into Kentucky, I became nauseous, and suffered bus motion sickness. The driver of our bus located a pharmacy, and Mr. Zumwalt went inside and purchased Dramamine for me to take. Within a few hours I felt fine.

While in Nashville, we visited the Ryman Auditorium. We stayed several nights at the historic Hermitage Hotel downtown Nashville. My roommate was Sharon Ewens from church. She had a twin brother, Dennis, who was also part of this group.

We moved on to visit the home of the late Andrew Jackson, the seventh president of the United States, who was also known as "Old Hickory." His home is known as the Hermitage, which had also been a cotton plantation.

Leaving there, we were on our way to Chattanooga and to the Great Smoky Mountains several hours away. After an amazing day, we returned to Nashville and to our hotel. We attended the church of our choice the next morning, saw the sights, and began our trip home on Monday morning. We arrived in Moberly late, after 11 hours of travel that day, but none of us missed classes the next day.

The school year was nearly over, with just a few weeks remaining. I was soon to be 18 years old. At that time, my dad would cease to receive a monthly Social Security Benefit for me. It wasn't much to begin with, and now there would be nothing. I always felt badly that my parents had to struggle, however God took care of them and they never went without necessities. I questioned why it was easy for some, and yet so difficult for others.

I had previously made plans to once again spend the summer with my sister and her family who lived in Independence, Missouri. As soon as school was over I left; however this time I rode with my brother-in-law's younger brother, Wayne, who drove a small red Triumph convertible sports car. This was a new experience for me. I had never before ridden in a convertible.

We spent the summer working, and playing. Being around my nieces was a joy, and I worked at teaching the oldest two the newest dance moves, and we all laughed. We took walks, and played with the neighbor kids. This seemed to be a neighborhood with young families and a number of children. I still had time to hang out with some of the teenage girls whom I had met the previous summer. In my spare time, I babysat for several of the parents, earning extra money.

On Sundays I typically attended Calvary Baptist Church, not far from where my sister lived. She drove me and picked me up afterward. There was also an RLDS church at the bottom of the hill as we drove along Spring Street into the Kentucky Hills neighborhood. One of the teenage girls in the neighborhood was a member, and she invited me to attend. At my church in Moberly, we had studied different faiths, and RLDS was one of them. Being curious, I really wanted to attend and see for myself, so one Sunday I walked the short distance to attend.

I was invited to sit with the young people, and they were friendly. Of course I knew Kathy. They asked where I lived, and that afternoon I was outside when a car drove up. There was a young man behind the wheel, he pulled over, and I recognized him as one of the young men at the RLDS church that morning. His name was Charles, Chuck for short. We talked, and he invited me to go to the RLDS Campus in downtown Independence that evening for a youth event. I went, and soon we began seeing one another; however I was too grounded in my Baptist faith to want to be part of any other faith. Chuck lived in the eastern part of Kansas City, not far from Independence, but he had driven to Independence for this special day at the RLDS

Auditorium. He was a nice guy, so along with attending the event, we also discussed our faith and beliefs.

Toward the end of summer, I made a decision that I would stay in Independence and finish my last year of high school. Since I was now 18 years of age, my parents left that decision up to me. I only needed a couple of credit hours to graduate, so I could work on the C.O.E. Program. It was a Co-operative Occupational Education program, which simply put, would allow students to be released from school for part of the day to work, while still receiving credit for doing so.

I applied for a job at Katz Drug Store, and I was hired. I would be working in the Sundry Department, but I would also work in the area next to it where records were sold. A number of teenagers came into the store to purchase records, so it would also be my duty to keep the popular songs playing most of the time, sort of as an advertisement. At that time, we could buy a 45 record for much less than a dollar. I began work each day at noon and worked until around eight-thirty that night.

I enrolled in William Chrisman High School as a senior in the fall of 1963. I had to get up early each morning while everyone else was asleep, so I wasn't able to spend as much time at home. I got dressed and walked down the hill to catch the school bus at the end of the street. After class, I walked from the high school to Katz Drug Store, which was on the Independence Square. By the time I got off work it was eight-thirty. Chuck would usually come and pick me up, and then we would drive to McDonald's or Smaks Drive-In, and get a burger and a Coke, and afterward, he would drive me home. I wasn't with my family very much, and this was becoming exhausting.

After about a month or so of this routine, I became tired and frustrated, wondering if I had made a mistake. Soon I wanted to go back home, so perhaps my decision to stay beyond summer was not what was best for any of us. I did not like the big school, I had no friends, and I didn't have much time at home. I knew when the weather started getting cold, I would have to walk to work from school each day, even in the snow. What if school was canceled, and I could not make it to work? I didn't want to be an inconvenience to my sister and brother-in-law, and yet I knew if I went home, I would have to get a job and help my folks. I did not want to quit school. I had held that diploma as my goal from the very beginning. I had seen the jobs that kids had to do without an education, and I didn't want that. So many decisions became overwhelming.

The more I thought about it, the more I prayed about it. What should I do? Wisdom was what I needed. How could I have ever thought that I could do this by myself? I needed God to give me guidance and I needed it soon. I had talked to my mom and I had moved my belongings from my sister's house and rented a room close to work on the Independence Square, paying for the room by the week. I was only there to shower and sleep, but at least it was close to work. Within a few months, it would be winter. I continued to walk to school each morning. A few days later, around the middle of October, my brother, now out of the Army, drove from Moberly and informed me that he had come to take me home.

Mojuco Car Wash

$1.50

Saturday, April 14

From 8 a.m. to 5 p.m.

COLLIER'S SHELL SERVICE

Cor. Williams and Carpenter

Fill up with gasoline too!

Sponsored by Mojuco Singers

Mojuco Concert Tickets May Be Purchased Now

Tickets for the annual Mojuco Singers Concert, to be held at 7:30 o'clock Tuesday night in the Municipal Auditorium, are now on sale. They may be purchased from any member of the Mojuco group. The price is 75 cents for adults and 50 cents for children.

ELEVEN

Home Again

AT HOME, I registered once again for school, and I tried to find a job. I knew if I stayed there, I had to work. There was nothing available except full-time jobs in factories. If I took any of those jobs, when would I find time to go to school? To my way of thinking, when a child reached adulthood, they were expected to contribute or be on their own. Because I was now eighteen, the Social Security benefit my dad was receiving for me had ceased. I was ready to quit school and get a full time job.

To solve this problem, the husband of my oldest sister stopped by our house on his way home from work. He worked in Moberly for the railroad. He told me to have my things ready the next day, and he would stop and get me and take me home to stay with them so that I could at least finish school. There were only seven months remaining. They lived only 20 miles from Moberly. My sister worked, so I could help out with the youngest daughter, plus I could also help with the house work, and the cooking. My niece, Betty was 15 and her brother, John, was 13. Phyllis was the youngest, and she was 11. I was going to share a room with Betty, which was really a good thing, because we were both close with one another.

Since my brother-in-law worked for the Wabash Railroad out of Moberly, and was gone from home during the week, he came home on Friday evening for the weekend. My sister worked at a uniform sewing factory in Glasgow Missouri, which was about 15 or so miles away.

I registered to attend school at Salisbury High School, and began my classes. There were a total of 32 senior students, so this was quite different, but I made friends quickly. There was not much for teenagers to do around Salisbury except to park on the square, listen to music on the car radio, go bowling, attend high school basketball games, and visit Andy's Drive-in Restaurant. That was our "go to" spot. My new friend, Donna was sometimes able to borrow her dad's car. He was a local barber, and they lived in an apartment above his shop. He was strict, so she could not stay out very late.

I joined the basketball pep squad, so when the team was playing out-of-town, I rode the bus to the games with the rest of the squad and cheerleaders. I had never actually been on a pep squad, but this was fun. This felt like home, and I was enjoying it. As we returned from our out-of-town games, and reached the city limits, we always began singing the school song.

We carried a sack lunch because the school had no cafeteria. The only thing they sold was milk. At home I was responsible for packing lunches. At school, we either ate on the grounds, or inside the gymnasium if it grew cold or had inclement weather. After school, I came home to be there when Phyllis came from school each day, and then I would begin dinner. Sometimes if Phyllis went home with a friend, Betty and I had enough time to walk the two blocks to the Rexall Drug Store and have a Coke before starting supper.

In Home Economics, we sewed some very challenging clothing. One of the garments was a fancy gown, and our second garment was a two-pieced lined suit. Our teacher was Carol Scheiderer. She was unmarried, and she dated Coach Moore. If we were cooking, and we needed items from the store, she handed her car keys to one of the girls and asked them to make a trip to the IGA grocery store for her. We thought she was pretty cool. She also set up tours of the homes of the prominent families in town for our Home economics class to visit. Sometimes the ladies of the homes would not only show us their home, but their china and silverware patterns as well. This became a custom for the seniors who were enrolled in Home Economics.

I was able to get a job working at the Ben Franklin Store on Saturdays for Bill Hollis. I became friends with his daughter Barbara, although she was a year behind me in school. I later worked as a waitress at Sterns Café. Since my sister and her family were members of the Methodist Church, I began attending church with them. The town was small, so everyone knew everyone else. Several of the ladies with whom I worked, also attended the Methodist Church. I felt comfortable at this church, but there was still a spot in my heart for Union Avenue Christian Church in Moberly.

It didn't take long until I was fully immersed in the Drama Class, and I also joined the Thespian Society. Several of the boys in class were class clowns, and they played a few horrifying tricks on the teacher. I won't spell out the tricks, but I chalked it up to the fact that the large number of these boys were farm kids, and a little bit more outgoing than city boys.

The music program for the school was lacking, and not quite what I was used to, especially with my passion for music, but that year I did participate in two drama productions. One of those was Shakespeare's "Midsummer Night's Dream." We had to create our own props, so there were many evenings that we spent at school creating backdrops. I became friends with Charlotte, who was quite a gifted Thespian. She was also skilled at doing dramatic readings. We also had a friend Laura, and the three of us became inseparable. Charlotte was allowed to borrow the family car, so she would pick up Laura and me to go to practice. We usually ended the night going to Andy's for a Coke before going home. Charlotte was an amazing girl, who wanted to be a nurse. From what I understand, she achieved her dream, and after nursing school, she moved to Chicago and became an administrator over a number of nursing programs.

I made a dreadful decision to lighten my hair by using "Light and Bright." After all, I had seen it advertised on "Dick Clark's American Bandstand." As it turns out, this was not a good idea, because it turned my hair clown orange. Phyllis took one look at it and yelled, "Aunt Bobbi, its orange!" I just kept shampooing until some of it lightened, and eventually it washed out.

Many important things happened that fall. The assassination of J.F.K. took place on November 22, just short of him serving two years as the U.S. President. I was working in the school office the day we received the word.

We all sat in silence and shock. On the day of the funeral, televisions were set up in the gymnasium. Students were free to roam around the gym and converse while watching the news, but we could not leave the gymnasium except to go to the office or the restroom. We watched the entire news coverage. It was such a sad day. Those are the momentous times in one's life when they always remember where they were, and what they were doing when faced with tragedy.

Our Home Economics class made enough cookies for the entire student body, and on the final day before our Christmas break, we served cookies and punch to the students and the staff during the last hour of school. Now it was almost Christmas, and my brother came to take me home for a few days. It was good to be with my mom and dad again, and to see a few friends, and even attend church. This was quality time, because it was about to get busy for me. I was also going to be starting a new job as a waitress at Sterns Café.

My sister's family planned to spend Christmas with her husband's family, so I planned on going to Moberly and spending Christmas with my parents. I was to be receiving a refund on my Income Tax from 1963, so I planned to used it to purchase my yearbook and graduation announcements. I had already purchased my senior pictures, because my sister insisted on loaning me the money to pay for them, and I was to pay her back when I received my refund. These things would be the remnants of my senior year. I framed my larger pictures and gave them to family as Christmas gifts.

When the second semester began, I was enrolled in Driver's Education. It was now or never. I was afraid if I did not get my driver's license now, I might not have another chance for a very long time. Mr. Roach was our instructor. We sat in class for a few weeks to learn the basics before his taking us to actually drive. Following the basic instructions on rules of the road and signs, he took us to get our driving permit, and then he began taking us out in groups of three. Each day, Monday through Thursday, we rotated turns, so each day a different group went with him, while the others remained in class during that hour with a substitute. The groups that remained in class watched defensive driving films and discussed what they learned. On Friday everyone was in class together, going over the criticism and discussion of that week before starting over again the next week. The substitutes were parents who volunteered their time, one hour a day, since the class only met for one hour each day, four days a week.

It was during the hands-on driving instructions with our specific group that Mr. Roach sometimes asked our driver to stop at the Ben Franklin Store where I worked on Saturday. He asked if I would mind going into the store to buy him peanut clusters. Of course he knew I would also receive a discount. He shared them with us, but most of them he kept for himself.

The car we used in Driver's Education was a 1963 Ford Galaxy. Each day Mr. Roach arranged for only one of the students to drive, and for the other two students to observe and take notes when we noticed something the driver had done wrong. When we saw something they had done well, we could also comment positively. There were 12 students enrolled in Driver's Education that semester, so there would be nine students in class each day for four days, and three students in the car with Mr. Roach. I was 19 when I became a licensed driver, and that was one week before I graduated. Mr. Roach went with me to take my test, and I was able to use the Driver's Education car in which to take the test.

In February 1964, there was a musical group that appeared on the "Ed Sullivan Show." This male group from Liverpool, England made a mark on the hearts of many people. Suddenly the Beatles were everywhere! While working at Ben Franklin, we suddenly had boxes full of all sorts of Beatle trinkets, including wigs. We could hardly keep enough records in stock. They sold out as quickly as they were unpacked. You could hear, "I want to hold your hand" in every café and soda shop in Salisbury, as well as on the radio.

We ate our lunch in the gymnasium during the colder weather, so the principal allowed the students to use the stage to dance to whatever appropriate music we brought to school. The school had a record player, and one person was given the responsibility for playing the records on any given day. We played Beatles music the most, with the Beach Boys coming in a close second. Mr. Menke said the exercise would do us good, then he would smile.

It was time to start thinking about the spring music contests. I had at least one arrangement of music that I was sure I wanted to use, but I needed a pianist. Betty Hollis, the wife of Bill Hollis, my boss, agreed to work with me. We began meeting several afternoons each week. The Hollis family also attended the Methodist church in Salisbury, so we met at the church during the afternoon to practice. The arrangement I had selected was "Mira" from the musical "Carnival" composed by Bob Merrill. I asked her if she had any suggestions for the second arrangement. She selected "Everywhere I Look," which was a lighthearted number composed by Molly Carew, and authored by Dena Tempest. We practiced several times a week. Betty was also a voice instructor, and she certainly knew the music that would receive a good rating. She didn't charge me a cent for taking on this task.

Our school went to Kirksville, Missouri, for the District Spring Music Contest. The day we went also happened to be the first day of spring. I was in a room facing a panel of judges, and behind the judges were large windows. The snow was coming down heavily. I made it through my first number just fine, so I thought I would have some fun with the next song. I announced my song and the composer, and I began singing lightheartedly with a smile on my face, "This morning in the merry merry wood the trees with laughter shook. They'd seen old winter hobble by, while leaning on his crook. The crocus called good-by to them, and the violets from the nook, for spring is here in fields of green everywhere I look." Then came a very light, "hahahahaha." The judges all knew how much it was snowing, and how spring had played a trick on us, and they began to smile as well. When the number ended, I looked at Betty and she winked. I think she felt good about it. I took home a number one rating. I also participated in several ensembles that day, plus singing with the school choir.

At home, John had just turned 13. Rubbing his chin, he said to his dad, "When do you think I should start shaving?"

His dad said, "Wait a minute," and went to the refrigerator bringing back some cream. While holding John down, he began rubbing the cream on John's face. His dad called for the cat, who promptly arrived, and began to lick the cream off John's face with his rough tongue to which we all began laughing.

His dad said, "This is the way a razor blade feels. Do you think you're ready?"

John shook his head, "No."

A month before graduation, I was offered a music scholarship to Cottey College in Nevada, Missouri, which was a two-year Methodist based women's college. This was quite an offer, but I really needed to seek guidance, and weigh my options. Actually, I did more asking of myself than asking God. It takes quite a while for some of us to let go and let God do things. Yet, during the next seven years, I would come to realize that.

I came up with every excuse that I could possibly think of; I have no money, so how will I pay for incidentals? I don't have transportation, so how am I supposed to get back home during school breaks? If I did go home, which home would I really consider home? Finally, I thought about this for several weeks, and I decided to forego the scholarship. After I graduated, I planned to go to Kansas City and get a job. My friend Joyce and I planned to get an apartment together. She was my friend from Independence, and she had already suggested this to me. This would prove to be a huge mistake.

Baccalaureate was held the second Sunday night in May. The following week was senior's week, so I didn't have to attend school that week. Neither did I go on the senior trip with the class, because I couldn't afford to take a trip. Instead, on Monday I went back to Moberly for the week to be with my mom and dad before leaving for Kansas City. I rode a bus from Salisbury to Moberly, spent the biggest part of the week, and then rode the bus back to Salisbury in time for graduation on Friday night. I also brought some of the items I had been saving in the paper barrel. We graduated on Friday night, and my parents were unable to attend. I said goodbye to my family and friends, and with my diploma in hand, and my driver's license in my wallet, I took a Greyhound Bus to Kansas City the next day.

Most of my belongings were already packed into boxes, so the bus driver stored them in the area next to the luggage. I was so appreciative of what my sister and brother-in-law had done for me by making all of this possible. During the ride I closed my eyes and tried to focus on what things God might have in store for me. I had at last made it, but it was sometimes a challenge. I was just a bit scared of what might lay ahead to say the least, and living in a large city was going to be very much different. What would be next for me? Joyce had borrowed her mother's car to pick me up, and she was waiting on me when I arrived at the bus station. We had a lot to talk about.

It had been a rough few years, and I often felt like a man without a country, jumping from one place to the other just trying to survive, but God had brought me through it. I knew there were choices that I had made that I probably should have done differently, but during some of those times I had to do the best that I could do, day to day, and trust that God would care for me. I was determined to graduate and receive my diploma.

Joyce and I moved into an apartment in Kansas City, and I began looking for a job and trying to make friends. Joyce taught me how to ride the Kansas City transit system, or the city bus line. I went back to work for Katz Drug Store, but this time it was in South Kansas City. Joyce went to work for

One-Hour Martinizing, which was a dry cleaning business. We spent most of our money to pay the rent, and it would be a week or so before we received a paycheck. We ate fried Spam and eggs the entire week. We rode the bus back and forth, and then I changed jobs and began working at Sydney's Restaurant on the Plaza, which was much closer to home.

I worked the late shift until closing. I was making 95 cents an hour as head waitress, but I was making at least 70 dollars a week in tips, and sometimes more. This was a considerable amount of money, but the problem was that I was spending it on myself. I was not going to church and I definitely was not giving God His portion. I tried to justify this action by sleeping late on Sunday mornings, making no effort to even find a church.

Joyce and I moved into an apartment along Main Street in Kansas City, closer to the Plaza. We rented a basement apartment, and since I worked the afternoon shift, most days I would take a book to read, along with my transistor radio, and spend a few hours across the street at the J.C. Nichols Fountain. Joyce worked the day shift at the dry cleaners. I got off work at midnight and walked the two blocks home. Joyce was often still up, and she begged me to go with her across the street and wade in the fountain, retrieving coins that others had thrown into the water. I was afraid that a patrolman might catch us, but it was difficult to see any active motion, because the lights for the fountain were turned off at midnight. Joyce was a fun loving girl, but also very gutsy, and a risk taker. She had a boyfriend, Tommy, who still lived in Independence.

This was when my battle began. My life became so busy that I no longer had time for God. I no longer opened His

Word and let Him speak to me. I put my personal desires ahead of His, and I believe I was really running from Him. I wasn't wild, and I didn't party, but none of my friends went to church, so I stopped going as well. I began dating, and fell in love, but I had failed to seek a man with a heart for God. He was not a Believer, and over time, he became physically abusive to me.

Psalm 46:1 NKJV says, "*God is our refuge and strength, a very present help in trouble.*" Soon God became the only thing in my life that I could depend on, and who was my unchanging, unfailing constant, because I had nothing else, however this was not without battle. I was unsure that I could even share my greatest fears with my parents, but all of this was realized over a period of time, when at last I did share with them.

Things did not work out as I had expected between Joyce and me. Joyce lost her job, and she was expecting me to pay the rent, and furnish the groceries. Her friends came to the apartment and ate the food that I had purchased. On a daily basis, there were more of her friends than I cared to deal with. My brother came to visit, and upon seeing that we had no groceries, he went just a few blocks away to the Blood Bank and sold blood so that we could eat. This was a great lesson for me, and Joyce and I parted ways. Although I felt the loss, I was okay with that. Afterward, I saw her only a few more times.

I'm not proud of some of the things in my life over the next few years, or the choices I selfishly made. After realizing my failure to follow God's leadership and what He had planned for me all along, I confessed my bad decisions to Him and asked Him to forgive me, but even doing that, took time. Some things we are willing to surrender, and some we actually want to keep. At last when I completely surrendered to Him, I felt a peace. Psalm 32:8 NIV tells me "*I will instruct you and teach you in the way you should go; I will counsel you with my loving eye on you.*"

I have chosen to leave out some of the details of my story, because I want to focus on the positive and uplifting things and to give the glory to God. I do know that over time, God broke this fragile jar of clay, and as I began to search, He created a new vessel. He assured me that I was valuable, because my value was in Christ Jesus. I had heard so many times that I was worthless, and I was beginning to believe the lie. I spent every minute I could possibly spend in His Word, and He began to speak to me. I found myself praying for a purpose for my life, and to be willing to do whatever He wanted to honor Him. I had the perfect plan, but that was my plan, not God's plan.

Several years later as a broken woman, God gave me understanding, and I began to strengthen my walk with Him. I remember many godly principles taught to me throughout my childhood by my mother and other Christians who had guided me in my faith. I remembered how God had taught me things about compassion and the human heart, and if He is abiding in our heart, and we believe His promises by faith, then we have all the power we will need. God also taught me much about forgiveness; however I had an enormous task ahead of me to discover that even for myself.

Just because we reject something that God has planned for us, does not mean that He tosses us aside. He always has another plan. After all, He is God! He knows us from the inside out, and from the beginning to the end. Are we glad of that? I'm an organizer by nature. I love to make plans and to-do lists. I like to be in charge, but my plans never work out quite as well as God's plans do.

Jeremiah 29:11 NIV says, "*For I know the plans I have for you,*" declares the Lord, "*plans to prosper you and not to harm you, plans to give you hope and a future.*" This is not a promise to instantly rescue us from need or suffering as much as it is a process. It is also a promise that God has a plan for our lives regardless of our current situation, and He can work through all of the ugliness to give us a hope and a future.

There is so much more to my story than this. My true ending is just my beginning. It is an ending that speaks of me becoming a single mother of two wonderful daughters while living seven years trapped in abuse, but even that is also a beginning, because it is a story of God drawing me back to Him after disobedience, and my failure to make Him first in my life.

God had a perfect plan for me, just like He does for each of us. Although I had always trusted Him, this is a story of how I cried out to God to deliver me by blessing me with a job so I would be able to support myself and my two daughters. By His faithfulness, He did exactly that.

It is a story of how God allowed me to find love and nurture in a man who loved God more than he loved me, and who told me I could never be number one in his life, because his Heavenly Father held that position. He told me however, that I could certainly be number two. It is a story of me uniting with a man in marriage for 37 years, and building a home where God was the head. Glenn and I were married on November 24, 1971. He went to be with Jesus on November 7, 2008.

EPILOGUE

OVER TIME GOD restored my passion for music, and although I was not able to obtain a degree, it does not mean that He was not able to use me in Christian ministry and bless me with positions of leadership in music. Glenn and I served God together for 37 years before he was called to his home in heaven. During those years, we witnessed many things transpire, not only in our lives, but in the lives of our five daughters. These years weren't always easy, but we faced the trials together and trusted God for the solutions.

We worked together no matter what it involved, whether it was raising animals on the farm, building fence, or baling hay. We did it together, and God also blessed us by giving us the strength to build two homes with our very own hands. That was such satisfaction to realize our help comes from the Lord, maker of heaven and earth.

Glenn was a man of many talents, and he was skilled in many areas. He was also the father of three daughters older than mine, and he was the step-father to my two daughters. We never had children together, but we were blessed to see each of our daughters mature, marry, and have children of their own. Neither of us ever referred to them as his daughters, or my daughters. They were our daughters. We have walked with each of them in their sorrows, and we have celebrated with them in their joy.

Together we became grandparents and great-grandparents. We were blessed to not only have five daughters, but we also have 13 grandchildren. A year ago, our oldest granddaughter suffered a crippling muscular disease and went to be with Jesus. By the end of the year 2020, we are expecting the birth of two more great-grandchildren, which will increase the number to 21. Throughout our time on earth, God has certainly filled our lives with abundance.

After the death of my husband, I poured myself into leading other women in God's Word. A few years ago, I suffered vocal cord damage, so I can no longer sing. God replaced my passion for music with a passion for His Word, and He has used me and blessed me lavishly. The importance of doing this is a huge command in preparing others for whatever God has prepared for them, and no matter what their need might be, their solution can be found by trusting Him. I have found the more I encourage others, the more God encourages me.

In the text of Isaiah 41:10 NKJV God tells me, "*Fear not, for I am with you; be not dismayed, for I am your God; I will strengthen you, I will help you, I will uphold you with my righteous hand.*" Throughout my life I have, indeed, experienced the "Blessed Assurance" that my mother would so often whistle. Whenever I think of this being my story, and being my song, I am reminded of two of His precious blessings that I have not only experienced, but which have guided my life from childhood. These are undeniably His *Echoes of Mercy, and Whispers of Love.*

The End

Printed in the United States
By Bookmasters